The Curse of Teko Modise

The Curse of Teko Modise

Nikolaos Kirkinis

Email: nikolaosmichaelkirkinis@gmail.com
Instagram: @k_nasty_8

Disclaimer

The conversations in this book have been constructed by Nikolaos Kirkinis after listening to Teko Modise recounting events in his life and career, so not everything would have been recalled verbatim.

First published by Jacana Media (Pty) Ltd in 2017

10 Orange Street
Sunnyside
Auckland Park 2092
South Africa
+2711 628 3200
www.jacana.co.za

© Nikolaos Kirkinis, 2017

All rights reserved.

ISBN 978-1-4314-2576-1

Cover design by publicide
Set in Sabon 11/15pt
Printed and bound by ABC Press, Cape Town
Job no. 003146

See a complete list of Jacana titles at www.jacana.co.za

*To the potential of South African footballers;
may we one day realise it …*

Contents

1. Teko, the street kid 1
2. The lady of the house 6
3. 'Who is Doctor Khumalo and how do I become him?' 10
4. King Tsiki Tsiki 16
5. Lying Steve 25
6. 'Say goodbye to your friend, Teko' 32
7. 'Ria is not going to call you' 36
8. 'I don't want to go to City Pillars' 40
9. One step closer to Bafana Bafana 45
10. SuperSport United 52
11. 'Orlando Pirates will change your life' 59
12. 'South Africa needs you, Teko' 68
13. 'The family I never had' 77
14. The move that wasn't 81
15. The number 10 that wasn't 86
16. Joel Santana 93

17. The World Cup 100
18. No wedding cake 105
19. The organisation 110
20. The king from Congo 117
21. The ridiculous suit 125
22. A rocky start 130
23. 'Downgrade everything' 138
24. Meant to be just friends 144
25. The legend from Barcelona 149
26. Pitso is in the building 153
27. The sun goes down 168
28. Making history 174

Epilogue: Not so cursed after all 178

CHAPTER 1

Teko, the street kid

Every man carries with him a set of mistakes to look back on. Among all the mistakes that Teko Modise made, he counts buying an Aston Martin as one of the biggest. It was a beautiful car, though, an Aston Martin DB9, just like the one James Bond drove.

He was going through a rough patch, and the car seemed like one of the only gateways to happiness for him. The 2010 World Cup had come and gone, and the nation was heartbroken. After all the hype and hysteria, Bafana Bafana had not lived up to expectations.

Teko sat in the parking lot of the Orlando Pirates training ground shortly after being told he was no longer allowed to drive his car to practice. He had fallen out of favour with his club. It felt to him as though his coach was his enemy, the newspapers were running an endless stream of stories about his recent public and messy divorce, and to top it off he had developed a nasty daily drinking habit. Teko was preparing to drive his Aston Martin to the bottle store on his way home. As his hands gripped the leather steering wheel he gazed at them and studied his scars and tattoos. He took a moment to consider where they had taken him, and the many things these hands had been through.

It made him think back.

Back to a time when these hands now holding the steering wheel of a R2-million car had dug through dustbins to look for food. He was eight years old at the time and his father had just kicked him out of the house and onto the street to fend for himself.

But perhaps this is already too far into our story. We should start even earlier, right where it all began, before he was a street kid, and long before he became the greatest South African footballer of the modern era.

Teko Modise was born in December 1982 in Meadowlands, Soweto, a low-cost housing suburb developed during the apartheid era to house black residents forcibly removed from Sophiatown during the 1950s and 1960s. His parents' marriage broke down when he was too young to remember, and Teko stayed with his father, Steven Sekgaila. Although his mother lived nearby, on the same street, Teko had no interaction with her during those early years.

As Teko recalls, his father did not have many friends, and in order to get out a bit he used Teko as an excuse to go to football games. Father and son bonded over the game: they didn't chat much in the normal course of things, but when it came to football, they couldn't stop. Steven was a Kaizer Chiefs fan, and so was Teko. His father used to tell him about all the Orlando Pirates and Kaizer Chiefs players, and Teko learnt all the players' names from his father: Neil Tovey, Lucas Radebe and Doctor Khumalo were spoken of as gods among men. He really liked that his old man took him to the games and that the one thing they could chat about was football, but the instruction was clear: talk about it, don't play it.

Teko's father was a strict, principled man who expected much from his son. For Steven Sekgaila, schooling came first and football came last. Although Steven had been a capable player in his youth, he disapproved of Teko wanting to play football and didn't allow it.

Young Teko took to playing football behind his father's back, as he could not stay away from the football field. Not only was the game an important part of township life; it also quickly became an important part of *Teko's* life.

From a young age, his talent was obvious and he was noticed early on by a number of local club coaches. The coaches would approach Teko separately and ask him to join the junior ranks of their clubs. Teko explained the situation, making it clear that his father didn't allow him to play. Thinking that Teko would be allowed to join as a junior if they could convince his father to change his mind, three of these coaches decided to visit Steven together one Sunday. As Teko recalls, 'That was the first and one of the biggest mistakes of my life.'

When the three coaches entered the house, Steven learnt for the first time that Teko had been playing football against his rules. The men tried to explain what a brilliant player Teko was, but the information was not received well at all.

'After they left, it was hell. I was beaten for inviting strangers into the house,' says Teko.

Steven was not the kind of dad whose wishes were easily disobeyed. Teko remembers his dad as a violent man, who often beat his son, even though he would never shout or raise his voice in anger at him. Steven had cut the cord that connected the kettle to the wall – a thick cord with copper inside – and this he then used to whip Teko. Sometimes the young boy had to go to school with long socks to cover the cuts and bruises that marked his legs from the whippings.

'It happened almost every day. I got beaten for everything and nothing at all,' remembers Teko.

As a youngster, Teko really paid the price for playing football. As part of a youth team, Teko had to take his own kit home to wash it. Although he would always try to wash his kit when his dad was out, sometimes he got caught and got a whipping.

'To be honest, though, through all the bad things my dad did, the one thing he made sure of was that I never missed a day of school. He couldn't help me with the work but he made sure there was always money for me to get educated.'

Steven worked as a petrol attendant in Midrand. 'But he always had a bit of cash lying around so I doubt that's all he did for money. He was a shady guy,' Teko recalls with a chuckle and a smile.

'He was the kind of guy who, when he walked out the door, you never knew when he was going to come back. Today? Tomorrow? I could never lock the door once he left.'

One hot day in December 1990, Teko's life changed. In the afternoon, Steven stumbled through the door with a huge cut on his head. It was a nasty wound. His clothes and body were all covered in blood. Teko had no idea what had happened to him but it looked bad and he was frightened.

Soon after that, Teko's father began to act out of character. Three days after returning home covered in blood, he told Teko to get his bag and pack all his clothes into it.

Teko had one big bag and he knew he could fit all his possessions into it, so he did as he was told. When he'd finished packing, his dad told him to leave his house.

Teko took a moment to consider what his dad was saying but he knew he wasn't joking. His dad never joked.

Steven kicked Teko out and, shortly afterwards, he locked the door and left the house as well. Teko was scared for his life; the one thought he had was to find his mother, but he had no idea what she looked like or where she might be.

Next door to Steven lived some family members from Teko's mother's side. In this house, they had a number of young boys and girls roughly Teko's age, but when he asked if they would take him in, they refused, telling Teko that there was no space for him.

'I think that was more painful than actually being kicked out. It was not like I was kicked out of home and nobody knew. Everybody knew, but nobody did anything about it. They acted like the whole situation was normal. There were kids my age sleeping on the floor of that house and they couldn't find room for my small body. These were people I knew were my family but wouldn't help me. That did the most damage to me mentally. What would happen if I died out there on the street? No one would have cared.'

Teko had to make a plan. He hid his bag behind his father's house and set out to find a game of football to play. It was here, at this game, that Teko met Peter. As it turned out, Peter was in a similar situation to Teko. He was supposed to be living with his grandmother, but because of the chaos in the household, he had moved out and had been on the street for a while. After Teko explained his situation, Peter decided to take him under his wing. Peter went with Teko to fetch his bag and then showed him the ropes of how to survive on the street.

In the day, Peter would take Teko to Florida Park. It was during the December school holidays, so there were many people picnicking in the park. Most of these people wouldn't finish their food and Peter would show Teko how to go through the dustbins to look for leftover scraps. Leftover chicken bones were considered a luxury. If they did not get enough food in the day, the two young boys would steal a bottle of cooldrink and try to sell it for R5 so they could buy some bread.

When the sun set and the park emptied, Peter and Teko slept in a hole by the side of the road nearby. In the morning, they would put their bags in the hole, cover it with cardboard, hoping no one would steal their belongings, and then set out again for the park.

When the boys weren't hustling for food, they played football. Teko always had a group of friends who wanted to play, and all the young boys they played with had dreams of one day playing for Bafana Bafana. However, once the game had finished, Teko did not want anyone to know he was a street kid, so he would only go back to the hole to sleep at night when everyone had gone home and there was no one to see him.

Thankfully, Teko didn't live on the streets long. His mother had not been in town when Steven kicked him out. Upon her return, she caught word of what had happened to her boy and she set out to find him.

Of course, Elizabeth Modise found her son playing football. She walked up to him, and as he looked up at her, he noticed that she had tears in her eyes. She had delivered this boy into the world but they were strangers to each other. Nevertheless, he knew straight away that this was his mother and she apologised to him for what he had been through, offering to take him in.

Teko had found a home, but his problems were just beginning.

CHAPTER 2

The lady of the house

When Teko's mother took him in, he thought that life would become a little lighter.

But after finding Teko, his mother wanted to perform a number of spiritual rituals on him: 'With me sleeping on the street she thought that I had come into contact with evil spirits.' The rituals had to do with Teko rubbing some unidentified substance all over his body. He remembers whatever it was causing unbearable itching, so much so that he would scratch his back against the nearest wall soon afterwards.

A more long-term problem was Teko's great-great-grandmother (khokho), who was the matriarch of the family. From the moment Teko walked into her house, he could tell it would be no easy ride. Not only was she ruthless in her efforts to raise a disciplined family, but the lady of the house took an instant disliking to Teko. It soon became clear to him that this side of the family resented Steven so strongly that Teko bore the brunt of it, just for resembling his father.

If you're thinking that it's odd for Teko to take on his mother's surname, you would be right. He did try to keep his father's surname, but shortly after moving in with his mother she made him change it. His father's name was banished in the house.

When Teko was brought to live in khokho's house, in Zone 7, Meadowlands, he met his aunt, as well as his brother David and sister Kgomotso, for the first time. He had heard of his older siblings but had never met them. They were from a different father.

All these family members lived under the same roof, but Teko was always the outsider. At this age, Teko felt he was the same as his siblings, wanting to play, run around and be silly. Teko tried to continue life as a normal kid. But this is difficult when the elders in the family treat you like an unwelcome visitor.

His childhood thoughts began to change slowly. He went from wondering when his next game was to much more serious questions like: What's gonna happen today? Am I going to get a beating? Am I going to get shouted at for something I didn't do? He just didn't know. Teko's khokho made sure he never settled in. He was constantly stressed as a child and admits that he never felt relaxed while growing up. All these thoughts were too much for a kid to process. As Teko puts it, 'As a young boy, to think a lot is not good; it makes you feel caged and alone.'

'I felt like an outsider in that house. Trust me, they did everything to make sure I felt like I did not belong, like a stranger in the family. It was hell,' says Teko.

Life had not been easy when Teko lived with his father, but it was a lot tougher with his mother and khokho. Steven may have been a strict and at times violent man, but Teko always knew where he stood with him; he always knew what was expected of him. His father's rules were clear-cut. The line was less obvious in his new home and he was in trouble every day.

Growing up, Teko also had a strained relationship with his brother. He describes David back then as more of a punisher than a brother. Thankfully, Teko's sister, Kgomotso was kind to him. She has always been and continues to be his only rock in the family. Kgomotso used to help Teko with his homework. She was the first person in the family to watch him play football. She attended all his games. When he was still an amateur, she would catch four taxis from Dobsonville to Diepkloof to watch him play. David only started to watch Teko play when he had signed for Orlando Pirates later on in life. Then, David enjoyed his younger brother's popularity. Teko cannot recall a time when his mother was in the stadium, even when later in his career he became captain of Bafana Bafana.

Teko holds no feelings of resentment towards his brother for their relationship as youngsters; he knows they were both children and knew no better. All his feelings of bitterness are reserved for the head of the house, his khokho.

But this toxic environment seemed to extend beyond the house. Teko explains, 'There was something wrong with the street I lived in growing up; I don't know if it was just my street or also others but it was never peaceful. Everybody hated each other. The only people who got along in the family were the kids and the only time we had peace is when we could play football in the streets. It is a strange dynamic, growing up in the hood … The families really were at war, though. This family would think the other had bewitched them and so on; it was absolute chaos. Then again, it is very rare to find a family in the township that functions properly.'

At least Teko still had football. He remembers football as his escape, his happiness and his release: 'When we played we were happy, but then, as the sun went down, we knew we were going home to problems.' Football was the only part of his childhood that kept Teko going; with a ball at his feet, he could be young. He may have been assured of a beating at home, but no one could beat him on the field.

When he wasn't on the football field, Teko felt alone in the world. He got used to being isolated and this made him pretty quiet as a child – in contrast to his brother and sister who were loud and excitable. They began to think that Teko didn't like them because he was so quiet and scared to join in whatever they were doing. He himself began to ask some questions about their differences: Why are they happy? We have the same mother; why they are filled with such joy and I am not?

Not only did Teko feel a lot of resentment from his family growing up, but he later felt even more unsettled as his mother moved around Soweto with him quite a lot, depending on job opportunities or the location of her lovers. This meant Teko struggled to build any lasting friendships.

The lady of the house

Finally, they moved to Diepkloof, which became Teko's saving grace. The place was football mad, with an abundance of talent.

On Sundays, Diepkloof came to a standstill. Township tournaments were, and still are, more popular than the professional league. It was here that Teko began his path to greatness. Teko would spend the next few years with friends who would go on to play for Bafana Bafana.

CHAPTER 3

'Who is Doctor Khumalo and how do I become him?'

There was only one football pitch in Diepkloof and it was the place to be on a Sunday. There were many teams in the area; some, of course, bigger than others. The biggest team would always play at three in the afternoon, when the sun was the hottest, the crowd the biggest and the pressure the heaviest. Teko wanted to play for this team, the first team, with the oldest, biggest and toughest players, but, unfortunately, he was a very small kid. Very small and very young. The coaches took one look at him and laughed; it looked like he had no place on a football pitch. Most guys in the team, Diepkloof Coventry, were around 18 years old, five years older than Teko.

Teko responded to their laughter, saying, 'Okay, I won't play with you guys. Just let me train.' They agreed.

After two days of training, they put him in the team. Two days was all it took to convince them that dynamite comes in small packages.

Teko's family moved to Diepkloof on a Tuesday; that very Sunday he was playing football in the biggest team in the area. He didn't know how big the game that week was. He didn't really care – given his mother's history, he didn't expect to stay in Diepkloof for long, so it didn't really matter.

'Who is Doctor Khumalo and how do I become him?'

During that week's game, he was brought on as a substitute. That's when everything changed for Teko. He performed wonders on the field.

Teko enjoyed talking about football with grown-ups; they always knew things that he didn't. At that time, all he heard from any adult was one name: Doctor Khumalo.

Doctor this, Doctor that. Doctor was a legend, immortal in football terms. He was a saviour, an operator, a magician.

Teko could see the joy that came to people's eyes when they spoke about this legendary Kaizer Chiefs midfielder. The Doctor brought joy to people who did not have much to eat or money to spend. They did, however, have their idols, and Doctor Khumalo was the most worshipped among them.

'Whenever people speak of Doctor Khumalo, you can see in their eyes that they mean what they say; he was everything to the people of South Africa,' Teko recalls.

So Teko began to idolise someone he had never met, someone whose face he could not even picture. He started asking, 'Who is this Doctor Khumalo? And how do I become like him?'

At the time, because of his success as a youngster on the township football field, Teko was becoming a household name in the area. At 14, he was already famous, even if only locally.

But he was famous only in Diepkloof. Because he attended school in Orlando East, which was a few of kilometres away, no one there knew that he was a good footballer.

'I would only really play football at school if I had no money for lunch. When you are playing you can't really feel hunger because your mind is on something else, so I even played football as a replacement for food.'

Otherwise, he would play for money, persuading some of the kids with a bit of cash to bet on the game. Teko would usually walk away with the proceeds. He was embarrassed, though, that he stayed in a shack, unlike many of the other kids in his school, so he would often wait for everyone to leave before he started walking home.

Things did not stabilise at home; his mom and her lover were breaking up. Teko was sick and tired of moving from house to house; he was sick of getting introduced to all these new guys. But, yet again, they moved. This time they moved to Orlando. He liked it there; he had friends.

Even though Teko moved, he stayed with Diepkloof Coventry in his old area.

His coach at Diepkloof Coventry was a good man named Kenneth Ngobeni, who used to buy Teko food after games. Teko's mother recognised in Kenneth a potential role model and food provider for Teko. And so she wrote to him, asking him to adopt Teko for a while. He agreed, and Teko moved in with Kenneth and his wife. Teko was, once again, a stranger in a family.

Kenneth encouraged Teko to do anything he could to succeed as a footballer. He pushed him to attend every tournament he could in the hope that he would catch the attention of the scouts.

In South Africa, there is a quip that goes: 'There is your age, and then there is your footballing age.' Many jokes are made that the player you are watching in the national U23 side may in fact be older than your father. This happens for a number of reasons but the main cause is that a younger player gets bought for more money, signs longer-term contracts and can postpone the uncertainty that comes with life after football. Age may just be a number, but when it comes to football, it is a currency.

Many of these players who fake their age get found out at some point in their career, which ultimately brings their life as a footballer to a premature end. The unfortunate thing about age-faking is that it happens so early on, before a player is mature enough to make a wise choice.

It is here that we can tell two different stories about two future Orlando Pirates players, standing on a bumpy field in Soweto one fateful Sunday as young teenagers. One of those boys was Teko Modise; the other one was nicknamed Little Napoleon or, more commonly, Tso.

Benedict 'Tso' Vilakazi is one of the shortest (1.57 metres to be exact) South African footballers to have ever played. He is also one of the greatest South African footballers to have ever lived.

'Who is Doctor Khumalo and how do I become him?'

Tso would become one of the top goal scorers of all time for the 80-year-old football club, Orlando Pirates; an impressive record that still stands at the time of writing.

Teko and Tso would both go on to be successful footballers but the two boys made different decisions that day that would stick with them individually right until the end of their careers.

All Tso's problems started one fateful Sunday in Soweto, when he was due to play alongside Teko.

The tournament was seen as a mini-national competition for Diepkloof. The area of Diepkloof was separated into various zones that were numbered. Tso was from Zone 2, but everyone in Diepkloof had been speaking about this skinny youngster from Zone 6 called Teko Modise.

Because Tso's team, Diepkloof Hellenic, was one of the best in the area, they recruited the best players, so they needed this young Teko Modise. Eventually, they found him and dragged him to an U15 tournament. These tournaments were very important because it was usually at an affair like this that a boy like Teko could find himself being scouted. This would be even better news for Kenneth, Teko's current coach and temporary guardian, who stood to make some money off Teko being scouted. The whole situation made Teko nervous.

The first issue was the field. The problem was that it was covered in grass.

'I was not used to playing on grass. I was a gravel guy,' explains Teko.

This tournament was more formal than other township competitions and, therefore, to play in it, you needed to prove your age.

This was a problem for a boy like Teko who had moved from parent to parent and shack to shack. He had never seen his birth certificate.

A man was walking around 'helping' the various teams. He noticed Teko's predicament. Many of the other boys did not have birth certificates either and those who did have the certificates wanted the numbers on them to be changed. All this man needed was the go-ahead and he would disappear and come back a few hours later with a new ID.

When this man returned, the IDs would still be hot – literally, hot off the press. These IDs were so new that the plastic on them would still be stuck together and the different IDs would have to be peeled apart.

Teko was amazed at how many wrongly aged boys were playing in this tournament. The issue with a business arrangement like this is that the deal is permanent.

Your new ID had your photo, name and birthplace. Everything was accurate, except for your birth date.

The permanence and shadiness of the deal scared Teko off, so he decided not to play with Tso that day. Teko wanted to be a great footballer but he wanted to do it the right way. That move helped Teko in his career more than he would realise at the time. Tso's career, however brilliant it may have been, was constantly rocked by scandals. If he was not involved in a sex scandal, he was involved in an age scandal. Accusations of his age-faking followed him around for his entire career and continue to haunt him today.

At a later tournament, Teko's team was about to take on Tso's. They were both captains. Teko refused to play. He walked up to Tso, saying, 'Chief, I was there that day. I know what happened. We not gonna play you guys – you guys are over-age. Most of you here have fake IDs.'

Teko left the tournament grass that day without spilling a drop of sweat. He returned to Kenneth to tell him the news. His guardian was not happy. Teko was taking up space and costing him money. He was a talented young boy but what use is talent in the township if you can't sell it?

Kenneth was growing impatient. He was prepared to do anything he could to cash in on Teko's talent. More than that, he just wanted to get rid of Teko so that he could live with his wife in peace. Once again, Teko was unwelcome in a home.

What frustrated Kenneth the most was that Teko hated going to trials. He hated trials more than anything. There were no fewer than a thousand boys vying for a handful of positions, and they each got a maximum of 10 minutes to show what they were worth. If no one passed you the ball that day then, as Teko puts it, 'You were out of luck'.

Kenneth wanted nothing more than to get rid of Teko, but this was difficult. He couldn't exactly return Teko to his mother; he had not heard from her since her letter. After that, she had disappeared without a trace.

Times were dark, and Teko's future seemed uncertain.

The only bright light was that the Brazilian national football team was on its way to play Bafana Bafana. This trip would have an impact on every boy in Soweto. Teko was no different. He was about to meet his heroes, and even though he did not know it at the time, he was also about to meet his competition.

CHAPTER 4

King Tsiki Tsiki

The year that Brazil came to South Africa was exciting for South African football lovers. The year was 1996 and Teko was 14. The Bafana Bafana of 1996 was a very different team to the one of today.

Bafana Bafana was a powerhouse, a continental monster that ate its enemies one by one. The team was truly feared. It may be difficult to believe, at the time of writing, given their current performance, but at that time South Africa was ranked first on the continent and nineteenth in the world.

This was the time of giants: Doctor Khumalo, Shoes Moshoeu, Mark Fish, Eric Tinkler. These men were walking legends.

Still, Brazil arrived on our shores expecting to teach South Africa a footballing lesson. No matter how great you are as a footballing nation, you will never be Brazil. While South Africa was celebrating being number one in Africa, Brazil was celebrating being number one in the world.

On the night Brazil played South Africa in April 1996, the atmosphere was electric. For most of the South African spectators, it was the greatest 45 minutes of football they had seen in a very long time. It was the kind of football you hear about in barbershops but rarely get to see with your own eyes. No one could actually tell the difference between South Africa and the world champions; they seemed indistinguishable in ability. The Brazilians brought the samba; the South Africans brought the shoe-shine. The Brazilians danced; the South Africans *diski'd*, a term used to describe feisty football, played with arrogance and agility. Each country had its own style, but both were beautiful.

Doctor Khumalo was something truly magnificent that night. In the 25th minute, the Doctor lined up a corner. Soweto was pulsating with excitement, as anything was possible with the ball at Doctor's feet. He sent the ball wide and high; it met the head of Phil Masinga. Bafana Bafana were up 1-0.

A couple of minutes later, Helman 'Midnight Express' Mkhalele made a dash down the right wing, crossed it outside the box, where it met the thunderous boot of Doctor Khumalo, who slotted the ball into the far-right bottom corner. South Africa were 2-0 ahead against the world champions.

Unfortunately, the second half was more indicative of South Africa's footballing fortunes: much promise followed by much heartache. Doctor was substituted in the second half and Brazil won the game 3-2.

Although that game did not result in a victory for Bafana Bafana, it did achieve two things: it showed that we had potential and it set off a wave of footballing hysteria around the country, particularly in the townships. Suddenly, the country became aware that there was talent to be discovered in South Africa; now it was just a simple case of finding it.

An aggressive campaign of recruitment swept the country. Trials were being held left, right and centre. Like a country preparing for war and pulling young soldiers from their mothers' houses, the football authorities began every effort to find the country's most gifted athletes.

Kenneth was growing impatient with Teko.

'You're no good, Teko, as useless as they come.'

'You'll never play for this Kaizer Chiefs that you love so much.'

'You'll never be as good as Doctor Khumalo.'

These words both crushed and inspired Teko. He was fearful that they may be true, but determined to make it not so.

'Going to trials is your only hope, boy. You need to get a move on. Look at Tso Vilakazi – he is already out of the hood and in a development programme. You are running out of time.'

So Teko went to trials in Orlando, not far from where he was staying. The trials were tough as the competition was stiff.

The coach of Teko's trial team was growing frustrated. All Soweto boys were the same, he thought. All they wanted to do was hold onto the ball and dribble; they wanted to be fancy and tricky. Like pickpockets at a Rolex convention, they wanted to embarrass their opponent and disappear with the ball. It was what attracted the crowds in a township, but it was also a coach's worst nightmare. You see, football is not an objective science; it is more a balance between art and science. And what seems like beautiful football to one man may appear barbaric to another. In the townships of South Africa, tricky and artful football is highly regarded. However, for most coaches trying to create a professional outfit, controlled football, based on discipline and structure, is the top priority.

'You guys don't know football. Tomorrow I will show you,' the coach said. 'Tomorrow I will bring a boy who will show you how to play football. I will show you football like you've never seen it before. I'm tired of all these dribblers. I need someone to control the tempo.'

The next day the boys started their usual business at trials. They were well under way, playing another game, when the coach interrupted them. The coach was late, but he had brought with him someone very valuable.

Next to the towering coach stood a diminutive and shy boy.

'Now, boys, today you are going to learn how to play football,' the coach said.

The small, shy boy was known in the townships as Yeye.

If the name Yeye does not sound familiar, you may also know him as Reneilwe Letsholonyane. If that name still doesn't ring any bells, you may remember him as the lanky midfield maestro with long dreadlocks who played for Bafana Bafana during the 2010 FIFA World Cup.

At the time Yeye was short and underwhelming. Teko looked at him and thought, who is this kid now? He's so short, he must be a striker. There was no way this small boy could be a midfielder. Teko knew all the midfielders in the hood; he had either played with or against them.

Teko stared at Yeye and Yeye stared back.

Neither of these two knew it at the time but these two boys looking at each other on a playing field in Soweto would go on to play in the FIFA World Cup, side by side, going toe to toe with the likes of Luis Suárez and Thierry Henry.

Yeye was and has always been a phenomenal midfielder. He played the same way at 15 that he does at 35. He was not like the other boys; he was not a fancy, tricky midfielder. He was pure class.

One. Two. Pass.
One. Two. Pass.
One. Two. Pass.

That was his style: less quantity, more quality. He controlled the game: slowed the speed when it was required and upped the tempo when the game needed some fire. His passing was so accurate, it actually frightened the other boys.

He was young but the maturity of his game suggested he had been playing top-flight football his whole life. After that day at those trials, all the boys in Soweto could not stop speaking about the young Yeye.

Footballers from the township were not supposed to play like Yeye. They were supposed to play shoe-shine football, fancy trickery, a combination of dancing and football, a style known as kasi football. This type of football is what moulded Teko in his younger years. Teko, too, was a tricky footballer; as was common when growing up in Soweto.

This style was personified best by a local legend named Thabo Mooki.

'Thabo Mooki was the king,' says Teko.

In Teko's eyes, Thabo Mooki is up there with the greatest men to have ever walked this planet. Thabo Mooki was the personification of what it meant to be a township footballer, to play with style and swagger. Mention the name Thabo Mooki in front of Teko Modise and he will cut you off with this sentence:

'Ah, the King of Soweto ... Kasi football ... He was something else, hey.'

Thabo Mooki was a professional footballer for Kaizer Chiefs. He played almost 350 games for the mighty Amakhosi. He is, without a doubt, a club legend. The Ryan Giggs of Kaizer Chiefs, if you will.

More than a club legend, he was a township legend. During the off-season, all the professionals used to duck out of their clubs after morning training to play in the township. It was their way of giving back to the community, but they got something from it too: they got to play free football, where they could express themselves, far away from their stern European club coaches.

Players were often nicknamed after famous songs or artists of the time. So later, Thabo Mooki earned the nickname Tsiki Tsiki, after a song by Kwaito artist Duncan. If you listen to the song while watching Thabo play, you will understand him and the township a lot better.

Everyone knew that Thabo Mooki's game was at three o'clock when the biggest crowd would gather around the stadiums. Thabo Mooki was the talk of the town.

For 15-year-old Teko to get to Moletsane, Thabo Mooki's township, he had to catch a train. He would go with one of his mates who loved football. Being broke, he couldn't buy a train ticket, so the young boys used to sneak onto the train however they could – hidden under something or riding on the roof of the train itself. Teko would always find a way.

Once, while making their way to a tournament, Teko and his friend got caught. A big, burly security guard grabbed the two boys by their scruffs.

'I would beat you, but you two are too small.' With two boys to mess with, the security guard chuckled to himself. 'So instead,' the security guard continued, 'I am going to let you beat each other.'

Teko was much bigger and older than his friend.

'I can't beat him,' Teko replied. 'I am much older than him.'

'Okay, fine,' said the security guard, pausing to think of a solution, 'then you two can just slap each other and I will let you go.'

The two youngsters stared blankly at one another.

'Either you slap each other, or I will slap you.'

'Okay, I will go first 'cause I'm older,' said Teko.

So Teko gave his friend a decent slap, but made sure not to hit him too hard. After all, this was his friend, a younger friend, and he didn't want to hurt him.

Then, WHACK! A thunderous palm to Teko's face. It was the kind of slap that gives you instant pins and needles in the cheek. The kind of slap that was as painful as it is was disrespectful. His eyes faced different directions for a moment and his jaw rattled. His friend had delivered an almighty smack.

The security guard was in hysterics. Teko was furious. He wanted to have another go at his friend now and give it all he had – not the half-hearted slap he had given him out of kindness.

The security guard had to restrain Teko, but eventually his anger subsided and they decided to move on. The train station was filling up and Teko knew that all these people were only here for one reason – to watch Thabo Mooki. If they didn't hurry, there would be nowhere to sit.

Teko and his friend argued the whole way to the game about that slap.

'Hey, man! Don't do that again! You ever slap me like that again and I will beat you properly.'

Everyone used to come to play against Moletsane, to try to test themselves against the king – Thabo Mooki. The boys even used to watch his team warm up, but often they wouldn't see him during the warm-up.

'Ag man, this is going to be boring. Mooki is not even here; this game is going to suck.'

Then Thabo Mooki would appear on the field, just in time for kick-off, seemingly out of nowhere. You would hear of his arrival before you could see him because the whistles would roar out of the stadium, so loud that they could be heard in neighbouring townships. Tsiki Tsiki had arrived.

The Curse of Teko Modise

The problem with the kasi football games was that they were very crowded. The youngsters got to sit in the front because they were the smallest, and the elders sat on chairs behind them.

Teko and his friends would sit on the side of the pitch until Thabo Mooki had the ball. Then everyone would stand up and cheer and if you were little there was no hope of seeing him doing his trickery.

'Thabo Mooki was a king. He was truly something else. Thabo Mooki used to embarrass everybody. Anyone who tried to take the ball off him would end up face down. He was too skilled for anyone to get the ball away from him. That ball was him. There was no one who could touch him,' remembers Teko.

Soweto is made up of various areas, and each area had at least one professional footballer who used to come and perform for his township. Brian Baloyi is from Alexandra, Teko Modise is from Diepkloof, Thabo Mooki is from Moletsane.

All the professionals from other areas used to come and see if they could outwit Thabo Mooki – some of the best players in the business: Thabang Lebese, Teboho Moloi, Jacob Lekgetho and Sizwe Motaung. They were all amazing footballers but none of them could match Thabo Mooki.

Teko has met Thabo Mooki many times since those days when he used to watch him as a child. The first time Teko met Tsiki Tsiki, he was star-struck. Even today he feels the same way. Teko would go on to play against Thabo Mooki as a professional in the Soweto derby.

Did Teko ever tell Thabo Mooki the way he made the youngsters in township feel? 'Of course,' Teko exclaims. 'Everyone told Thabo what he meant. He knows. In the hood, you bow to Thabo Mooki. He was the greatest township footballer of all time. You know when you are in the hood that you must bow to the king.'

Watching Thabo Mooki play on TV for Kaizer Chiefs and watching him play kasi football were two very different games. Those who got to watch him dribble and dance with the ball at his feet count themselves as truly fortunate. It was a completely unique style of football.

A professional player playing in the township was his way of staying true to his roots and inspiring a younger generation to make the best of a tough situation. If a youngster could watch someone grow up in the hood, go on to become a professional and then still find it in his heart to come back to the hood voluntarily, it sets the right kind of example.

That's exactly what Thabo Mooki did for Teko Modise. The lesson was not lost on Teko and he would go on to follow in Tsiki Tsiki's footsteps when he turned professional.

Pitso Mosimane, Teko's coach, would lecture them many years later, when Teko was playing professionally for SuperSport. He would warn them not to play kasi football. It was dangerous and could ruin their careers. The rocky pitch was a minefield for a professional footballer's ankles.

The players would only pretend to listen. There was nothing that would stop them from playing kasi football. They would train in the morning and then disappear in the afternoon to represent their townships, playing for nothing but pride and fun.

Teko got to play with and against some incredible players – both professional players in the stadiums and amateurs in the townships. But Teko still says the most impressive player he ever saw in the township was Thabo Mooki.

The next best was a lanky midfielder from Katlehong called Emmanuel 'Scara' Ngobese. The name holds celebrity status. Scara, like Tsiki Tsiki, played for Kaizer Chiefs, and such was the legendary status of the man that he was nicknamed 'Black Jesus'. Some said he could be mistaken for a darker Zinedine Zidane; others said that he looked like an ice-skater on the football pitch as he moved so effortlessly.

Scara was not only a legend in South Africa. Ask Paul Scholes of Manchester United about Scara and he will tell you about the time that Scara pulled a 360-degree body swivel while keeping the ball still, a move that had Scholes searching left, right and centre for the ball while Manchester United were playing Kaizer Chiefs during a pre-season tour.

Scara, like Thabo Mooki, was the hero of his township.

More than 10 years later, during the off-season, Teko's agent, Jazzman Mahlakgane (an important figure in this story, we'll get back to him later) recruited Teko, Scara and a couple of other players to play a township tournament in Polokwane.

Among the players recruited for the tournament was Orlando Pirates legendary midfielder Steve Lekoelea.

Steve was a joker. 'You were never serious if you were around Steve,' Teko recalls.

On the bus on the way over, Steve was sitting at the back, Scara was sitting in the front and there was no music playing. On such bus trips the driver either puts on his favourite gospel CD, or dead silence is the order of the day.

Scara and Steve were having a round of friendly banter with each other from opposite ends of the bus. There was much banter to be had; one was a Kaizer Chiefs legend and the other an Orlando Pirates legend. They were kings of Mzansi.

Teko remembers that Scara was coughing in the bus; he did not sound healthy. The mood was joyful, but no one in the bus knew it would be Black Jesus's last game.

Township football made people happy, especially when they saw their professional stars returning to show respect. It made the community happy but it came at a price. Steve Lekoelea would go on to be injured in one of these tournaments, effectively forcing the clubs to ban their players from participating.

As for Scara, well, he had been sick for a while. Teko thinks that the final game in Polokwane may have been too much for him. He was already sick and they were playing on a very dusty field in December. It was hot and dry, not easy on the lungs.

Scara passed away from tuberculosis a couple of months after that game. The nation lost a hero. Teko lost a colleague and a friend.

CHAPTER 5
Lying Steve

To carve an elephant out of a block of wood, start with a massive block of wood and chip away everything that is not the elephant.

This is how football trials in Orlando worked when Teko was growing up. Boys were being dropped by the day and coaches were refining their squads until they had what they believed was a respectable team. The pressure was mounting on Teko.

All his friends were being selected for the higher teams. Day by day more people around him were getting one step closer to the big leagues.

'When are you going to go, chief?' people used to ask Teko.

He had bigger worries on his mind: What if I get kicked out of home again? Where will I live? Do I have to become a street kid again?

The pressure of his insecurity all became too much for Teko to handle and he stopped attending trials. It was a heart-breaking decision; once he withdrew, all his friends started getting selected for the team. Teko deserved to be there but he was the master of his own demise. The team that was selected went on to play a tournament in London.

The period before the team left for overseas was the most painful for Teko. He watched the camera crews roll into Soweto, going from house to house filming the reactions of the players' proud families.

He watched the friends he used to chill with on the street corner getting new passports – legitimate passports from Home Affairs. He watched them get new bags, new kits and get interviewed for TV. He watched but did not participate.

What hurt the most was when they returned home. Travelling on a plane is something a young boy from the hood only dreams of. Teko had never seen a plane, let alone sat in one.

'How was it?' he asked. 'How far did it go? How fast did it go? How high did it go?'

Teko's morale was at an all-time low. Kenneth was on his back about being useless; everyone around him was making it big.

It was during this time that Teko met Steve Mnguni and his life began to change.

'With Steve Mnguni, you never knew if he was telling the truth or lying. Whatever he told you was never upfront.' This is Teko's reflection on the late Steve.

Steve and Teko would go on to share a complicated relationship. Steve would help Teko on his path to becoming a professional, but when Teko was famous, Steve exaggerated the role he had played to the media. Steve, until the day he died, claimed that he was the one who had discovered Teko Modise. This was a fabrication.

Steve Mnguni was a local businessman and heavily involved in football in the area. He approached the 15-year-old Teko one day and indicated that he wanted to start a team – a development team, a feeder team. A feeder team is set up for the purpose of finding young footballers and training them up for a specific senior team. Steve was charged with finding the best young footballers to feed to the professional outfit, Ria Stars, based in Polokwane.

Ria Stars was completely different to his expectations. The club was owned and run by Ria Ledwaba, a shrewd and tough businesswoman with short, golden hair. Their nickname was Manyora, meaning the Bosses. These days, Teko describes Steve Mnguni as shady, but that mattered little at the time. Steve told Teko what he wanted to hear; that he was a phenomenal footballer.

Not many people in Teko's life had been that forthcoming with affection towards him, so this was new. Steve sat him down and told Teko that he was brilliant.

'You're going to go professional,' Steve said. 'I'm going to build a team around you and you're going to be my captain. Once Ria Stars sees you, you will be the first player they buy.'

Teko was not surprised that he was chosen as captain of the new team. In most teams, he has found himself as the leader. Teko ascribes this to his upbringing.

'I was brought up in a very strict household. The dishes needed to be done at seven and not five past seven. I've carried that mentality to the field with me. I don't just say it, I also do it. If you are a defender, then your job is to mark. If you are a winger, then your job is to run and cross. If you are a striker, then your job is to score. End of story. Everyone has a job. Do yours, or pack up and leave,' says Teko.

From the moment Steve told Teko how good he actually was, the young boy became obsessed with football again. All Teko had needed was some motivation. All he needed was someone to believe in him or at least pretend to believe in him. And Steve really seemed to believe in him.

'We were buying the *Soccer Laduma* newspaper every week without fail. At break time, we would sit with our friends at school and read the *Laduma*. We would check the interviews to see who had said what.'

Teko and his friends changed their habits to match those of a professional footballer. They now went jogging and did extra fitness outside of training. Teko and his mates even started practising what life would be like as professional footballers, what they would say when they were one day interviewed by *Soccer Laduma*. They started speaking about how they should carry themselves and behave when they turned pro. Teko and his friends even practised their autographs and giving their signatures to youngsters. They decided that, when they were older, they would never leave behind a youngster asking for an autograph; they would make time for everyone, no matter how famous they became.

Teko wanted to be the kind of professional everyone loved. He particularly wanted the kids to love him, and he wanted to be that guy who always had time for his fans. Most of all, he just wanted to become one of the greats. He wanted to be greater than Doctor Khumalo.

Steve had got Teko and his mates excited about the big leagues, and gave Teko the authority to look for new players. Teko went on a recruitment drive through Soweto and found a number of talented youngsters. Steve made Teko feel special; he made him feel in charge. It was Steve's way of keeping Teko part of the operation.

The team was ready and the boys were keen. However, as Teko explains, you never really knew what was going on with Steve. He would organise a friendly game here and there, and then disappear for two months. He would return with excuses, saying he was sorry; he was in Polokwane or Tzaneen for this reason or that.

Teko's mates were growing tired of it all. 'When are our trials? Where is our kit?'

Teko had no answers for them. He didn't even know where Steve lived. One day, after being disappointed yet again, he decided that they should just forget about Steve and these false dreams of turning pro. They left the team, saying that if Steve wanted to find them, he knew where they lived.

In the meantime, Kenneth had finally had enough of Teko and kicked him out the house. Kenneth didn't evict him because he disliked the boy; it was simply becoming impractical to have him around. Kenneth had not known how long Teko would be staying when his mother initially dropped him off. He was taking up space and costing him money, and with Teko's reluctance to attend football trials, it was looking unlikely that he would make money off him.

But it wasn't long until someone else took him in. Teko approached a local man nicknamed Ace and asked if he could move in. Ace and his wife made a living selling alcohol from their house in the township. Ace was no stranger to Teko. In fact, Ace was one of the people who used to help Kenneth collect lunch money for Teko. Ace didn't take too long to consider Teko's request. Because the hood is small and people talk, he knew Teko was good at football and that he was not troublesome; he also had a spare bedroom.

As time passed, Teko realised that there were not many opportunities for a boy from the hood. He wanted to become a professional footballer more than anything. He was a good student but he saw that academics were not necessarily going to get him out of this place. There were others in the hood who did well at school and some of them ended up staying in the hood after school anyway. He didn't want to take that chance.

He also knew he had to find somewhere permanent to live. He knew he could not stay with Ace and his wife forever. 'If my own dad could kick me out, my real father, then what would stop someone else from kicking me out?' The situation was just not sustainable. His own family had never even bothered to check how he was. It was football or nothing.

So Teko began to attend trials again. He went to trials for the School of Excellence, a renowned soccer academy. At those trials, he saw some soon-to-be-famous players, including Steven Pienaar.

The trials went on and, day by day, Teko's friends were being cut. It got to the stage where he was the only boy from his area having to wake up at four in the morning to catch the bus to trials. Those trials opened Teko's eyes. He saw that guys like Steven Pienaar were now on TV, playing for the U20 South African side. He could see that the dream was achievable. Maybe if he tried, he could actually make it. He started doing extra training, trying harder than ever.

Eventually, one of his friends, who was playing for a team in the second division, Dobsonville United, invited Teko to come try out for the team. A legendary Kaizer Chiefs player, Fani Madida, coached the team at the time. Fani had been a goal-scoring machine in his day; he even played overseas in Turkey. It was the first time Teko had met a Chiefs legend.

Teko went and trained with the team. He was skinny and tiny, and even though he got kicked around a bit by the older guys he so enjoyed the camaraderie that he didn't really mind.

Fani approached Teko one day: 'Listen, boy, I would love to

register you but I can't. It is the wrong time of the season. I can only register you next season. I want you to come with for our next game, though. Come on the bus; I want you to get the feel for how it is to play a proper game.'

Their team was scheduled to play Black Leopards in Venda, Limpopo. The drive from Dobsonville to Venda by bus is a long, slow trip. Roughly 12 hours with its many stops. The whole team had to squeeze into one bus so they resented Teko's presence there. He was not even registered and here he was taking up precious space. Teko didn't care.

Later, the team lost the game to Black Leopards and this turned out to be a crucial game as Dobsonville missed out on promotion, and Fani Madida was dropped as the coach. This was a huge blow for Teko – not many coaches took a chance on younger players. Fani followed the signs to the exit and took Teko's dreams with him.

This was another disappointment for Teko, and becoming a professional footballer was becoming a more distant dream by the day.

One day, Ace sent Teko out to buy some bread for the family. As Teko dragged his feet back to his current home, he noticed a bus waiting outside the house. The bus was full of players and there was a man standing next to it talking to Ace.

The players in the bus were telling Teko to hurry up and that he was wasting time.

'I don't even play for this team. What do you guys even want from me now?' Teko replied.

That's when he noticed the man talking to Ace. It was Steve Mnguni. That deceptive Steve Mnguni.

'Come, Teko,' Steve said, 'get in the bus. Ria Stars is playing a game in Tembisa and my development team, here in the bus, are playing the curtain-raiser. Chicco and Ria [the two owners of the team] really want to see you play. Come, get in the bus.'

Teko stood back and crossed his arms. He had let Steve lie to him one too many times.

'There is no way. I am not getting in that bus. Knowing you, we will not even go to Tembisa; we will end up in Polokwane. We are probably not even going to a soccer match.'

Ace cut Teko's attitude short.

'Just go, Teko. We are not that busy today; we don't need your help around the house. Just go. What's the worst that could happen?'

Teko climbed into the bus, and that moment changed his life forever.

CHAPTER 6

'Say goodbye to your friend, Teko'

The developmental team went off in their bus, now joined by Teko. They were lining up against a strong Tembisa XI.

Twenty minutes into the game, Chicco Twala, co-owner of Ria Stars, stopped the whole game and pulled Teko off the field.

Chicco was no ordinary fellow. He was a massive deal. His full name is Sello Chicco Twala. A music producer, and a very good one at that, he was well known for his collaborations with Brenda Fassie, the 'Madonna of the Townships', as well as writing a number of songs that were used in Walt Disney's *Lion King II*. He also once co-owned the once-mighty Moroka Swallows.

And here he was, on a hot Saturday in Soweto, pulling Teko off the field after just 20 minutes.

Was I that terrible? Teko thought to himself.

'Go get changed and come sit with me,' Chicco said.

When Teko returned, he sat next to the big man in absolute silence.

'He didn't say anything. I thought Steve had put me in a terrible situation again,' Teko recalls.

After the curtain-raiser, they brought food for the boys to eat. Teko was so mad; he thought he had blown his chances again. He started eating ferociously. He was eating out of anger. He ate everything he could get his hands on: chips, pap, you name it.

Halfway through his feast, one of the senior players walked up to him.

'Hey, chief, you starting there.'

Teko looked up, with his food hanging out of his mouth. 'Starting where, boeti?' he asked.

'The first team. You're starting. Come get your boots. Let's go.'

Teko walked sheepishly into the change room. This was a PSL team, a big team with big players – the likes of Frank Makua, a Bafana Bafana midfielder; Lucky Lekgwathi, future legendary Orlando Pirates defender; and striker Joel 'Fire' Seroba.

Teko was overcome by immense feeling. There was hardly room for butterflies in his stomach, after his massive consumption of food prior to his call-up, but he was nervous anyway.

Teko played 45 minutes before being subbed off once again. Chicco had hardly said anything to Teko the whole day. After the game, he walked up to the young boy, pointed a finger at him and said, 'I'll come to your house tomorrow.'

That's all he said. But for Teko, who had been lied to and fed nonsense his whole life, this felt like just another empty promise.

The next day, Sunday, Teko was chilling in the hood watching a game. He was exhausted from the day before. A young boy had been sent to get him.

'Ace wants you,' the little boy said.

As Teko wandered back home, he noticed a white Mercedes-Benz SLK-Class parked outside Ace's house. He thought some rich man had come to buy alcohol. When he rounded the corner, he saw Chicco talking to Ace.

Ace was just ecstatic to have Chicco in his house; he did not care why he was there.

Chicco came with the story that he wanted to take Teko to Ria Stars. He promised that Teko would finish school in Limpopo and would be well looked after. Teko listened but didn't get excited. As far as he was concerned, this was just another promise that would probably end in disappointment.

'If it happens, it happens' is all Teko said to them.

The Curse of Teko Modise

'Tomorrow I will come to your school,' Chicco said to Teko, pointing an authoritative finger at him.

Yeah, sure, Teko thought.

The next day, Teko returned to school for the start of the week. As predicted, nothing special happened. The boys went to assembly, came back from assembly, and started class.

'You see,' Teko said to one of his mates, 'this guy is not coming.'

Ten minutes into class, the whole school was called back to assembly. Everybody. All 500 learners crammed back into the meeting point.

Teko was one of those boys who liked to hang at the back in these kinds of situations. He got bored easily when someone was making a speech.

The place was buzzing. Everyone wondered why they'd been called back and thought something was wrong. Perhaps someone had been shot or something had been set on fire.

Suddenly, Teko saw Chicco standing up in front of the whole school, next to the headmaster.

This was something truly spectacular. Chicco was an idol, and idols never visited a school like this. Ordinary people didn't know how to act around Chicco. Not even the principal could keep his composure. Standing at the podium, the headmaster started going on about all the things Chicco had achieved. He mentioned Brenda Fassie and Ria Stars.

When it was Chicco's time to speak, he got up and addressed the learners with authority.

Teko was shaking. He was hiding in the corner. He was so nervous. He was a shy guy, and this was his worst nightmare.

'I've got a surprise for the school.' Chicco paused and looked around. 'There is one boy here.' He paused again. 'One boy who plays football like I have never seen someone play football before in my life. I have a PSL team. I want it to be as big as Kaizer Chiefs and Orlando Pirates …' He paused for a long time. 'And I am here to announce that I am going to be taking Teko Modise with me.'

The school erupted. They all went crazy. This was the biggest thing to happen in a place like this. It was at this point that Teko

'Say goodbye to your friend, Teko'

realised what a mistake it was to hide at the back of assembly.

They called him up on stage.

'It was the longest walk of my life,' Teko recalls.

He had to walk through the mass of 500 students, all pulling, pushing, hugging, kissing and slapping him.

He got up on stage. Chicco put his massive arm around Teko. He smiled, looked up to the crowd once more and announced: 'Say goodbye to your friend Teko. This is the last time you will see him in the flesh. The next time you see him will be on television.'

CHAPTER 7

'Ria is not going to call you'

Teko refused to believe that his first PSL move had happened until the team bus came to fetch him. Even then, he had some doubt, but all of that flew out the window when the bus stopped to pick up Frank Makua.

When they signed Teko to Ria Stars, they told him: 'We want you to play exactly like Frank, in case he gets injured or something like that.'

Frank was everything to Teko. Teko studied Frank: the way he moved, the way he passed, the way he carried himself. Teko idolised Frank.

Ria Stars set all the players up with somewhere to stay. Teko was signed along with two other youngsters, one of whom was Green Mkhabela, who would become a close friend of Teko. Teko, then 17, was the youngest of the three.

That season was really difficult for Teko. For his first contract, he was signed for two years and paid R2000 a month. It was the most money he had ever had in his life, but it still didn't have the legs to last the month. He had to take the accommodation provided and was forced to pay R700 for rent ... On top of that, he had to have money for groceries and entertainment. His roommate was earning R16 000 a month. The older guys ruled the town. They had all the money and all the girls loved them. The younger guys, who were paid less, hardly went out.

'Ria is not going to call you'

There were also divisions in the team. Ria Stars was originally set up in Polokwane, so most of the guys were from the area. They spent their blood, sweat and tears getting Ria Stars promoted to the PSL and now felt it was unfair that just because the team was more professional, management had brought in a whole lot of 'foreigners'.

There were three divisions in the team: 'Polokwane guys, Joburg guys and foreign guys,' explains Teko. A 'Joburg guy' was anyone outside Polokwane but still inside South Africa.

As the season wore on, more and more of the youngsters got a chance to play. Teko was the only one who was excluded for a long time. He got his first run when Zimbabwean coach Shepard Marupe put him on against Wits University, the oldest white team in the country. Teko played 80 minutes and started cramping. The coach told him that he needed to train harder, which Teko felt he was already doing. But Shepard never used to sub Teko on; he only used to start with him.

Teko played eight games that season and then one day, out of the blue, they called a team meeting. Everyone was summoned, from the head coach to the water boys.

Ria Ledwaba stood in front of them and announced: 'We're selling the team.'

The PSL had decided to reduce the number of teams in the league from 20 to 16. They approached some of the teams towards the bottom of the log and offered them R8 million each to, in effect, disappear. Ria took the deal.

'Don't worry, we will find you guys new clubs,' Ria assured them.

Teko took her word for it, but he had his doubts. He had only played a handful of games that season, so he doubted any other teams actually knew his name. Ria, however, convinced Teko that John Comitis, the Greek South African owner of Ajax Cape Town, was looking at him.

Teko went back to Soweto to live with his sister, Kgomotso. He was unemployed and back where he started. Kgomotso had been the only family member who had kept in contact with him. By this time he had no idea where his mother was and his father was well and truly a thing of the past.

A while later when Teko was relaxing at home he got a call from Pitso Mosimane. Pitso was a young coach at the time but would later go on to become the Bafana Bafana coach. Even later, he became arguably the most successful club coach in South African footballing history. At the time, though, he was in charge of SuperSport United.

'Hey, Teko. I want you to come play for me at SuperSport United.'

Teko thought he was joking. SuperSport United had such quality players back then, there was no chance of him featuring.

'No, don't worry, just come,' Pitso said. 'I'll come fetch you every day and we'll go to training. Let's see if we can sign you.'

Pitso stayed true to his word and fetched Teko to take him to train with the team every day. Pitso wanted Teko to replace Thomas Madigage. Thomas remained a loyal servant of SuperSport United for many years as a player and a coach, until, at the age of 41, his car collided with a donkey in Limpopo.

Teko had big shoes to fill. Thomas Madigage was a legend at the time, as were his fellow players. They were a team of pure quality.

Teko felt he was in the same position as he'd been in with Ria Stars. He thought he was never going to get a fair chance to play, which is all he wanted to do. He was desperate to make it all the way to the top.

He trained with SuperSport United for one week, but he saw himself going nowhere with the team. He predicted another season condemned to the bench, so he ran away. He disappeared without a trace, not telling Pitso anything. Pitso arrived one day to fetch Teko for training and he simply wasn't there.

It was the first speed bump in the very long and complicated relationship between Pitso and Teko.

After he ran away from the team, Teko was at home when he got a call from Green Mkhabela, one of the other youngsters who had been signed to Ria Stars with him.

'Ria is not going to call you'

'Hey, chief, where you?'

'I'm at home, why?'

'What you doing at home?'

'I'm waiting for Ria to phone and sort out my contract.'

'My man, Ria isn't going to call you.'

'What do you mean?'

'Teko, Ria has sold our clearances.'

'Huh?'

'Ria has sold our clearances to City Pillars.'

'What the hell is City Pillars?' Teko asked.

'No, man, it's that team, you know, that one in Tzaneen that we used to play in friendlies sometimes.'

'Hey, wena! That team! No ways, there is no ways I'm going there. Ria said I'm going to Ajax.'

'My friend, Ria is not going to call you. You are not going to Ajax.'

What Green was saying turned out to be true. Teko tried to call Ria repeatedly but she never answered. It wasn't long before Teko got a call from someone else at City Pillars – a Nigerian defender called Sam Pam.

'Hey, Teko, you better come here.'

'I'm not going there,' Teko answered.

'Look here, boy, you can come here or not come here but the fact of the matter is that these guys own your clearance now, so they own you. Whether you like it or not, that's the case. If you don't come here you'll kill yourself as a footballer. Why not just come here for a season, impress someone in the PSL and maybe you can get bought by a big club?'

Teko was going backwards, back down to the second division.

CHAPTER 8

'I don't want to go to City Pillars'

The year was 2002 and Teko was heading to Limpopo.

'I don't want to go to City Pillars,' Teko complained. 'We used to thrash those guys 6-0 or 4-0 when we played them in friendlies. How am I supposed to get back to the PSL with those guys?' The truth of the matter, however, was that Teko had no choice. They owned him.

It wasn't all that bad, though. After speaking to one of the owners, he learnt of the quality players coming to join the team. Nine of the players from Ria Stars were joining, so there would be some familiar faces. Other players who joined included legendary Cameroonian international Roger Feutmba, Joel 'Fire' Masilela, and Kaizer Chiefs star Isaac 'Shakes' Kungwane, who once scored a goal directly from a corner kick and another time from the halfway line.

Teko started to believe in the team. City Pillars had ambitions and, with these players, they actually stood a chance of making it back to the PSL.

The owner put some money in Teko's account to catch a taxi from Orlando to Tzaneen. It was a very long drive. He arrived in Tzaneen to start his new life, now earning R14 000 a month.

'Just imagine. I had gone from earning R2000 to R14 000. I felt like a king.'

There was a problem, though: Teko faced tough competition for the number-10 jersey from the more experienced campaigners, Shakes Kungwane and Roger Feutmba. At the time, Roger's nickname was 'the General' – the same nickname that Teko would earn later on in his career.

But the players who knew Teko from Ria Stars warned Roger and Shakes: 'Hey, you guys are going to struggle for the number-10 jersey. This boy Teko is good.'

'Ag man, he is too young, too skinny. That's not a worry,' they would reply.

All the players, including Teko, arrived mid-week. That weekend, a friendly game was scheduled to showcase the players to the people of Tzaneen. It was a small town but City Pillars was a community team and was very well supported in those days. It had 10 times the support base that Teko was used to at Ria Stars.

In the first half of the friendly, the coach played all the big stars. The people went crazy; they did not often have superstars in their town. It was the first time they had seen the great Roger Feutmba in the flesh, having previously only seen him play in the World Cup on TV.

In the second half, the coach brought on some of the younger players, including Teko. The supporters were pretty disappointed with the move; they wanted to watch the stars all day long. They thought it was going to be a dreary affair.

Teko turned their yawns into gasps of disbelief. He played with the confidence of a superstar. He controlled the midfield, set players off on runs. There was no defender who could touch him.

From that day on, Teko Modise became a household name in the area. The season went on and Teko featured often. He was just starting to make some headway. City Pillars, unfortunately, missed out on promotion to the PSL that season, by one point. However, some of the other teams were beginning to notice Teko, so much so that some club owners took to depositing sums of money into Teko's bank account, not to bribe him, but just to be friendly and to be remembered in the future.

While living in Limpopo, Teko fell in love for the first time.

His first romance would develop into a seven-year affair with a young woman from a similar background to Teko's. Her name was Linky.

Linky was a local girl from Limpopo, and her family was refreshingly well balanced. Teko liked that about her; he was attracted by the stability in her home, so different to what he grew up with. Her family liked Teko too, often housing him, feeding him, and even lending him money when times were tough. Teko was lonely at City Pillars and Linky helped him through those times. It was a very comfortable relationship. However, they both knew that Teko was just at the beginning of his career.

At City Pillars he began preparing Linky, 'Listen, here's what's gonna happen. One day, I am going to be playing in the PSL. There's gonna be a huge hype about me. Ladies are going to throw themselves at me. I just want to tell you this so that you can prepare for such things and I hope that when it happens both of us will be mature enough to deal with the situation.'

Linky was one person Teko truly believed he could build a family around, with her at the centre. Linky was by his side in the dark, cold and poor days when he had nothing. She loved Teko for just being Teko.

The only issue was that Linky did not take Teko seriously when he warned her about the fame, bright lights and attractive women that come with being in the PSL. She never thought it could be so bad. She was a shy girl, and she wasn't prepared for Teko to become as big as he did.

Teko's issues with the women in his life did not begin and end with Linky. During his first season in Limpopo, he received a call. The voice on the other end of the line was haunting, yet familiar. It was his mother.

He had not heard from her in a very long time. In fact, their last interaction had been when she wrote Kenneth a letter asking him to take Teko in. Since that day he had had no idea whether she was even alive or not.

She had started seeing some pieces in the newspaper about a boy in Venda who was turning out to be a phenomenal footballer.

She realised it was her boy, and was encouraged by a friend to get in touch.

She told Teko that she needed to speak with him. It was an emergency, she said, so he decided he should go. City Pillars was so happy with the effort he was putting in for the team that they had bought him a Toyota Tazz. He drove all the way from Tzaneen to Orlando.

'Now imagine,' Teko recalls, 'it was a very tense situation. This woman felt like a complete stranger to me.'

When Teko arrived in Orlando, his mom proceeded to tell him that she was sick and had been ill for some time now.

Teko felt very angry at the news. He had many powerful emotions that flowed through him, and he felt that he hated her at the time.

'She was reaching out to tell me now that she was sick. She couldn't reach out to me any other time? There were times when I needed someone, anyone, to talk to. I needed someone to help me; I needed someone to share my experience; I needed someone to share my happiness, as well as my sadness. She dumped me as if I was nothing and then some six or seven years later, she reaches out to me to tell me she was sick?'

The whole experience left Teko confused, angry and disappointed. He got in his car and drove back to Tzaneen, crying the whole way.

No matter how eager Teko was to move forward with his life, his family problems followed him. While playing for City Pillars the next season, Teko got a call from his sister. His great-great-grandmother had passed away.

'Look, Teko, there is a problem. All these people are acting like they were not related to this lady. No one wants to put in money to bury her.'

And so it was that Teko ended up paying for the funeral of the person who had hated him most in this world. No aunt, uncle or even distant cousin contributed a cent. Teko approached City Pillars to ask for some time off and a little money to help with the funeral, which they gave him.

The irony was not lost on Teko. This was the woman who had made his life hell, and here he was, burying her and wishing her a peaceful journey to heaven.

'Regardless of how I felt about her, I felt like it was the right thing to do for the family to bury her, so I flew to Joburg and that's exactly what I did.'

Teko only cried at the funeral when he saw his brother, David, crying. It was hurtful for Teko to see his brother in such pain. David loved his khokho and she loved him back. Teko learnt through family members that, on her deathbed, right before her final breath, Teko's khokho uttered her final words: 'Go and call for David.'

While his great-great-grandmother may not have called for him, Teko buried her nonetheless. After the funeral, he got back to work.

CHAPTER 9

One step closer to Bafana Bafana

'I'm wearing a T-shirt with my surname on the back. Modise. It's a surname I'm not even proud of. I don't know where it comes from. I don't know my history. It is my surname, though. I can't change it, and today I want the whole of South Africa to know my name.'

Teko had big things ahead of him, and big things behind him. He felt like he was going somewhere but his family was holding him back. Now that his mother had his number, she would call him to ask for money for different reasons.

Teko didn't like it but he gave her the money anyway. He felt much frustration and anger. His mother had never offered her help, and now, when he was starting to make it in his career, she was often in touch.

The conflict and feelings of hatred Teko had towards his family only pushed him to work even harder. He wanted to make sure he was going to be a success. He never wanted to be on the street or even in his childhood house again.

'Let me just make it big. Just in case. Just in case anything happens, let me just make it big so that I have no regrets.'

Luckily for Teko, the perfect platform for just that was on the horizon. City Pillars were due to play Kaizer Chiefs in the 2006

ABSA Cup. The ABSA Cup allowed teams from all leagues to play against each other, and it was this that allowed the minnows, City Pillars, to line up against the giant Kaizer Chiefs. This was a once-in-a-lifetime opportunity for the boys from City Pillars to play the team that most of them grew up supporting.

The pressure was on. FNB Stadium was packed. The atmosphere at a Kaizer Chiefs game is unforgiving for the enemy. As Teko lined up in the tunnel to take to the field, he could hear the crowd roaring outside. He looked next to him and saw the legendary Shoes Moshoeu lining up for Kaizer Chiefs.

It was the second time Teko had been to FNB Stadium, and it was the second time he had met Shoes Moshoeu. The first was in 1996, when Brazil had come to play against South Africa. That was the same game that sparked the wave of trials and football mania across the country.

During that period, in 1996, there were two groups of young players from Soweto selected to train with the senior national teams. One group was sent to meet the Brazilians and the other to Bafana Bafana. Most boys wanted to go see the world champions, to be trained by the likes of Bebeto and Romario.

But Teko wanted to train with Bafana Bafana so that he could see Doctor Khumalo. When they arrived at FNB Stadium to see the national team, they all had to choose a player to do drills with. Most of the boys ran straight to Doctor: he was an icon – *the* icon. It was at that point that Teko's pride kicked in. He didn't want to be like the other kids, so he went up to Shoes Moshoeu instead; they did some drills together and then afterwards the stars chatted to the boys. Shoes signed Teko's T-shirt and his ball. Teko asked him for his boots, but Shoes gave him his socks instead.

Now, a decade later, they were lining up side by side, about to do battle on the field against one another.

'I knew Shoes would never remember me. I was a little boy who asked for his signature. But today I wanted him to remember. I wanted the whole of South Africa to know. Today was the day that newspapers would start typing out my name.'

It was game on. Teko played like a world-class professional, and the game turned out to be a nail-biting thriller. The match started predictably with Kaizer Chiefs going up 2-0 after 20 minutes. Things slowly started to turn around though, and soon after the halftime break, City Pillars were amazingly ahead 3-2. Both teams threw everything they had at each other and thanks to two goals from the young and unknown Teko Modise, the game finished 4-4. Shoes Moshoeu was among the goal scorers for Kaizer Chiefs and the game went to extra time.

Unfortunately for Teko and City Pillars, the fairy tale was not to play out to the end. Pillars goalkeeper Lucky Shiburi had an absolute shocker of a game. He was wearing six studs (the wrong number, given the conditions) and was slipping all over, as if he was playing with bars of wet soap for shoes. The game finished 5-4.

Despite the loss, that game changed everything for Teko. Suddenly, he was on the radar of all 16 PSL teams. As it became clear that Teko Modise was the next big thing in South African football, more and more people approached him, either to offer him something or to ask him for something.

An up-and-coming football star always attracts a football agent. Teko began his career managed by Alex Bondarenko, son of former Orlando Pirates coach, Viktor Bondarenko. For whatever reason, Teko and his agent were constantly banging heads and had few nice things to say to each other. Teko wanted to leave the National First Division (NFD) and make a big-time move to the Premier Soccer League and felt frustrated by the lack of progress.

The first time Jazzman Mahlakgane remembers laying eyes on Teko Modise was when City Pillars locked horns with Benoni Premier United at the 5000-seater Bidvest Stadium in Johannesburg in 2006. The game was an important one: it was the promotion/relegation playoffs, where the winner would be in the PSL limelight. The loser would be condemned to the black hole of the NFD. Teko's side were the losers that day.

The result, in the end, mattered little though. Jazzman had noticed a number 10 who was unforgettable.

'I remember seeing this boy. The first thing that struck me was that he had cornrows. I liked that; clearly, he was different to any other player out there. Most importantly, though, he was busy on the field. Like it was the last game of his life. He was involved in every aspect of the game: with corner kicks, he was there; free kicks, he was taking them. He wanted to win and you could feel it.'

After the game, Jazzman set out to find him. He looked all over the stadium but couldn't find this young boy named Teko Modise, who everyone was looking for that day. Eventually Jazzman found him hiding from the limelight in the parking lot.

At the time Jazzman was no big fish either. He had just started his agency and had only recently moved it from a room in his house to a tiny office in Parktown. If you walk into Professionalz Sports Management and Marketing today you will see a professional corporate setup. There are some impressive jerseys hanging up on the wall: those of Happy Jele, Siphiwe Tshabalala and Teko Modise among them. Jazzman has two boardrooms and even a massage parlour out back, next to the pool. He didn't start his career at this level, though. He worked his way up and he did so by spotting talent early.

When Jazzman eventually tracked down Teko, he did not have a big sales pitch, as is the custom with most agents. That is, ironically, what sold him to Teko. But there was one problem: 'I can't sign with you. I already have an agent,' admitted Teko.

They left it at that, but it would not be the last that Teko heard from Jazzman.

The season ended for City Pillars and, once again, they did not gain promotion to the PSL. However, it was a very fruitful year for Teko. Although he missed out on being the league's top goal scorer by one goal, he won the Player of the Season Award.

At the awards ceremony, Teko remembers feeling a little uncomfortable: everyone was wearing tuxedos and he was in a T-shirt. But he didn't care too much: he collected his award, grabbed his R10 000 prize money and disappeared to enjoy it.

Life was good in the off-season for Teko. He was a sought-after man. He was waiting for a deal from Kaizer Chiefs to come through. He had been talking to Bobby Motaung, the manager of

Chiefs, and things seemed to be going smoothly.

Still, it was usual for teams to send the coach or a club legend to present the offer. Chiefs sent a player by the name of Siphiwe Mkhonza, who had played with Teko at Ria Stars, to convince him to sign. Teko felt belittled and undervalued by this. He was even prepared to turn down an Orlando Pirates offer in favour of Kaizer Chiefs at the time, but Bobby's decision to send a player to convince another player had the opposite effect.

Orlando Pirates were playing beautiful football. A Serbian, Kosta Papić, was coaching them at the time. He used to sit on the side of the field, smoking cigarette after cigarette and yell, 'Attack! Attack!'

Teko almost signed with Pirates and the Serbian, but his sister convinced him otherwise.

'Start small. Don't go to these big teams just yet.'

'But I've been starting small. When is it my turn to go big?'

'Just go somewhere you'll be appreciated.'

So Teko took some time off to think. He still had the R10 000 from winning Player of the Season and he had just been given a new car, a VW Polo, from City Pillars. So, he used his off time to party.

The South African U23 team was assembled in camp at the time. There were always controversies with that team. They used to call Teko when they were bored: 'Hey, man, we bored here in camp. Come bring us some booze and sneak in.'

It was often the late Gift Leremi who would ask. Gift, as the name suggests, was an incredibly talented player. Unfortunately, he was killed at the untimely age of 22 when the car he was driving overturned on the highway in a gruesome accident.

Amid all this off-season partying, Teko received a call from Pitso Mosimane one evening. Teko stared blankly at his phone. This call was disturbing for two reasons. Firstly, Teko hadn't spoken to Pitso since he had run away from him and the team, and secondly, Teko hadn't slept in two days and Pitso wanted to meet that evening in Sandton.

When Teko went to meet with him, Pitso had a few angry words to break the ice. After that, he proceeded to tell Teko of his plans to use him at SuperSport United. He was willing to move beyond Teko's previous behaviour. He had a system in place that would guarantee Teko game time. On top of that, Pitso was set to be the assistant coach of Bafana Bafana, and with the 2010 World Cup coming to South Africa in four years' time, Teko wanted nothing more than to play for the national team.

The decision was an easy one, but the process was comical in its chaos. Teko called City Pillars to inform them.

'Hey, guys, I need my clearance. I'm going to play for United.'

'No, man, your clearance is not here any more. It's with Jomo Cosmos.'

'Jomo Cosmos …' Teko repeated.

He let out a little chuckle and then said it a couple more times under his breath.

'Jomo Cosmos … Jomo Cosmos … What the hell is my clearance doing with Jomo Cosmos?'

He found himself in the same predicament once again.

Jomo Cosmos is a team owned and run by possibly South Africa's greatest-ever footballer, the Black Prince of Soweto – Jomo Sono. Jomo used to sell peanuts outside the stadium as a young boy and was once called upon to play for Orlando Pirates when they were a player short on game day. He would go on to play in America alongside the great Pelé and Franz Beckenbauer.

Jomo had a knack for spotting and exporting talent, and he almost convinced Teko to join him. Jomo wanted to make a quick deal. He wanted to pay Teko R12 000 a month, which was peanuts compared to what Teko was after. Jomo Cosmos has also been relegated and promoted more times than any other team in the history of South African football, so you never really knew which league you would be playing in the following season as a Cosmos player. But Jomo promised to export Teko overseas.

The next day Teko was due to appear at his first training session with Pitso but he never showed up, unable to deal with the catch-22 situation he found himself in.

Pitso phoned him: 'Hey, man, you're up to your rubbish again.

You don't want to train!'

Teko had to make a decision and make it quickly. The whole thing with Jomo was happening so fast that it scared Teko. It was either overseas or Bafana Bafana. Teko decided to stick with SuperSport United. He apologised to Pitso for not coming on time to training, informed him of the issue with his clearance and left that problem for SuperSport United to sort out with Jomo Cosmos.

All that mattered was that Teko was going to Pretoria, and he was one step closer to Bafana Bafana.

CHAPTER 10

SuperSport United

SuperSport United was, is, and probably always will be one of the top teams in the local league. Their power varies from competitive to sometimes downright unstoppable. To this day, they remain the only team that has won the league three seasons in a row. Furthermore, the coach of Matsatsantsa is always closely tied to Bafana Bafana. Dressed in blue and white and based in Pretoria, SuperSport United is a good place to find yourself as a player.

When Teko Modise arrived at one of the bigger clubs in the country, there were some big names already there. Many of the players were still young but would go on to form the base of the Bafana Bafana team for the 2010 World Cup. Among the stars were Siboniso Gaxa, Thabo September, Ricardo Katza, Daine Klate and Katlego Mashego.

Many of these players were turning out for the junior national team or receiving debutant call-ups for Bafana Bafana. Furthermore, Pitso Mosimane was very close to the ear of the Bafana Bafana coach at the time, so if you impressed Pitso, you could impress the nation.

The players at SuperSport were young and raring to go. Most importantly, they were all friends, earned similar salaries, and managed the balance between partying and training.

At SuperSport United, there was no camp, meaning that the

night before a game, the players were not all required to stay in the same place, as is the custom with most other teams. During Teko's first season, a very important game was scheduled for a Saturday in July: Orlando Pirates vs SuperSport United. Naturally, Teko and his fellow players from SuperSport United were taking the game very seriously.

On the Friday before the game, Daine Klate threw a party for his fellow SuperSport United teammates. The team was very focused and, even though it was a celebration, they were only drinking Red Bulls or water.

Daine Klate had invited friends from other teams and Lebohang 'Cheeseboy' Mokoena, a fierce Orlando Pirates player, arrived at the party with a crew of Pirates players. Cheeseboy began joking with Teko and the other SuperSport United players: 'Hey, look at you guys. You are very focused. I can see you are taking this game very seriously, drinking your Red Bulls and waters. Tomorrow we will show you guys – we are going to beat you.'

Cheeseboy's announcement threw the SuperSport United players off slightly. They gathered for a conference at the party:

'Listen, guys, we can't lose to Pirates tomorrow. If these guys are drinking and carrying on they are probably going to be hungover tomorrow. We can't lose to them. We will be fine.'

The following evening, the game commenced. The SuperSport United players were fired up and hydrated. They fancied their chances against the reckless Pirates.

The very same Cheeseboy who was making jokes and boasting the night before the game came on as a substitute in the second half. He scored two goals to sink SuperSport United 2-0. Teko and his teammates were shocked.

'Whatever, gents,' Teko said to his teammates as they walked down the tunnel after the game, 'we tried our best. Now it's our turn to go out and drink.'

Upon signing for SuperSport United, Teko felt as though he had taken a big step forward in life. He was the only person from his family to graduate out of the hood. Now he was playing for a top premiership team, he felt he should give more back to his family.

Despite the tough upbringing they subjected Teko to, his sense of responsibility ran deep and he was aware he had to provide financially for his family, as he was the only one with the means to do so.

Teko approached his mother and offered her something big: 'Mom, can I buy you a house? Please let me buy you a house. I hate this home here in Zone 7. I will never feel at peace returning here. I want to be able to be happy when I say I'm going home. I want to be able to visit you in a proper home. Let me buy you a house.'

But Teko's mother refused the offer. She was happy where she was, in Zone 7, Meadowlands. She said she had grown up in that house and that was where she would remain. Teko, even when visiting that house today, is still haunted by his upbringing. His mother's reasons for refusing a new house made no sense to him. It made him feel that every time he tried to do something good for his family, it was rejected.

Later on, when his mother's birthday was approaching, Teko offered her another gift: 'Mom, tell me how many friends you have. Just tell me the number and I will book a bus for you. You guys can go to any restaurant you want. I will book out a section for you; no one will bother you guys. You can have the whole night, just you and your friends. You can eat and drink anything you want. The only time I will show up is to pay the bill.'

But his mother refused this offer as well. This relationship with his mother felt really complicated; now that he was trying to help, she refused his offers.

'That hurt me to the core. I tried everything to fix our family and was given nothing in return. I moved to Roodepoort to be closer to my family so that it was easier for them to visit me and for me to visit them. They came and visited me twice in six years. When I moved to Fourways, no one came to visit. When I sign for a new club, my sister is the only one who congratulates me. My family just see me as a walking ATM ...'

Teko was about four months into his contract with SuperSport when he and Pitso started fighting again. It was the first time that

Teko had well and truly been shouted at by a coach. In hindsight, Teko recalls, 'Maybe he just wanted to get the best out of me.'

Pitso didn't like who Teko chose as friends in the team. Katlego Mashego, Katlego Mphela, Siboniso Gaxa and Teko Modise would all go on to be some of the biggest stars to ever feature in Bafana Bafana, but at the time, when they all walked around together with their sagging pants, colourful kicks and fancy cars, they looked like trouble.

Pitso didn't want Teko hanging out with that crowd. Pitso felt they were a bad influence on the young man. The funny thing about it, though, is that Teko was one of the most influential in the group. He was no victim of bad influence; he was one of the culprits.

He would often say, 'Guys, let's do this, let's go here.' But Pitso wasn't aware of Teko's role in the group. He thought it would make Teko a lesser player if he continued to socialise the way he did but Teko didn't see the harm in socialising with teammates, at least they were all in it together: 'If we don't show up for training tomorrow, then we're all in trouble.'

They were in the same team coached by the same boss, so it was in their interest to behave and misbehave together.

As the season wore on, Teko's name became better known and spoken about more often in public. People began to say, 'Maybe this kid has what it takes; maybe he can make it in Bafana Bafana.'

Pitso was worried that all of this would go to Teko's head. At the same time, there was a player in Teko's position, Richard Rantjie, and the coaches were struggling to choose between the two. The problem for Richard was that Teko was very skilful, so he, Richard, was seeing more of the bench than the field. The problem for Teko was that SuperSport wanted Richard to extend his contract with the club, and in order to convince him to take this deal, they needed to play him more regularly. So, they benched Teko, temporarily. Pitso told Teko to take it as a sign that he should be working harder and partying less.

'I wasn't even partying that much. If I was then Siboniso Gaxa would be in real trouble. I was never worse than that guy, and the funny thing is that he was also the best player on the pitch.'

Deep down, all these young boys wanted the same thing – to represent Bafana Bafana in the World Cup. The issue was that they looked like trouble and that never sits well with any coach, especially old-school coaches.

However, their off-the-field connection helped them on the field. Footballers talk football and, often, over a beer, Teko would say to Katlego Mashego, 'Hey, why did you pretend like you didn't see me on the field today? You must pass next time.'

Next time, Mashego would pass and they would play better. It was a good system but it stank of ill-discipline.

The disagreement between Pitso and Teko had reached a level of pettiness. Teko was often held up as a bad example. One day, Pitso invented a team award, the 'Teko Modise Award'. The joke was that Teko had more sound system in his car than engine. This award came in the form of a monetary fine for any player who bought a car and then spent more time and money customising the sound system than anything more useful in the car.

'When Pitso is the coach of a team he can do whatever he wants,' says Teko.

Teko could take all the chirping and the comments. He was from a tough background and made of tougher stuff, but even he had his limits.

'There was one moment when Pitso did something that really made me say, "I don't care anymore".'

Pitso summoned Teko to his office. The late Thomas Madigage was also present. Pitso was complaining about some aspect of Teko's behaviour. It was a sensitive time: preparations for the World Cup were in full swing. Pitso looked Teko in the eye as they sat on opposite ends of the room and said, 'The Bafana Bafana coaching staff asked me about you. I told them you were not ready to play for Bafana Bafana.'

That one sentence absolutely crushed Teko. Pitso knew how badly he wanted to be a Bafana player.

'I told them you're not ready,' Pitso repeated. 'You'll only be ready when I decide you're ready for Bafana Bafana.'

If Pitso was intending on giving Teko a push with that statement, it had the opposite effect. Teko started to make friends in every shady corner of the country, from Hammanskraal to Tembisa. He started going in his own direction. He wanted to become the deviant that Pitso thought he was. He wanted to prove Pitso right. He didn't train as hard as he had before and as a result he was being played less often. If there was no prospect for Bafana Bafana then there was no point.

Teko simply could not understand the man's thinking. The confusing thing was that Pitso was not coming down as hard on the guys who were partying every weekend with Teko. Guys like Gaxa and Mphela were already in the national team and moved in the same social circles as Teko. But they were spared the wrath of Pitso.

'This was the man who came and fetched me when I was 18 to replace Thomas Madigage. This was the man who fought for my clearance when Jomo Cosmos took it. If you are the father in the household and your child does something wrong, you should not put him down and oppress him. Why not just correct him? Show him the right way?'

Pitso carried on telling Teko that he had a big head; he didn't like the way Teko walked and talked; his attitude suggested trouble. Teko started feeling as he had when he was growing up with his family: rejected and valueless.

For Pitso, another issue was that Richard Rantjie was even more badly behaved than Teko was perceived to be. Pitso had two players in the same vital position and they were both troublesome. Richard was unpredictable, a destructive guy off the field. He was often in trouble and would only train when he felt like it. Although very talented, he was unreliable.

This forced Pitso's hand into playing Teko more often, which was good for him, and then things changed some more when he met Vusi 'Computer' Lamola, who urged him to push harder. Anyone alive in the 1970s would have heard the name. Computer, as the name suggests, was an absolute genius on the field and remains so to this day. He was a vital part of the much-feared Kaizer Chiefs squad in the 1970s, winning the support of millions of South Africans. To this day, the club can thank men like Computer, Nelson 'Teenage' Dladla and Patrick Pule 'Ace' Ntsoelengoe for their continued support.

Computer made the team tick. He was mechanical and artful at the same time. He is the original South African midfield maestro. Extremely well spoken, he has a smooth voice and his words carry a special kind of wisdom. 'And when Computer speaks to you, you must bow,' Teko says.

One day, Computer approached Teko, accompanied by a journalist. Computer put a hand on Teko's shoulder, and said, 'You are a good footballer, son. A very good footballer, in fact. You are even better than I was. It's just that you don't realise it. Focus, my boy, and you will see how far you can go.'

The weight of the compliment crushed and comforted Teko at the same time. Here was the great Computer Lamola humbling himself to a nobody like Teko and telling him to push harder. So Teko did.

CHAPTER 11

'Orlando Pirates will change your life'

The drama between Teko and Pitso subsided a little and normal life resumed. Teko was playing regularly and the news that Pitso would be leaving SuperSport United come the end of the season was filtering through the grapevine.

Pitso was to be replaced by Gavin Hunt, possibly the most feared and respected coach in the local game. He took no nonsense. He has been described as a rugby coach in a soccer coach's body. He swears and shouts, but he gets the best out of his players. When SuperSport United made history by becoming the first-ever South African team to win three PSL titles in a row, it was Gavin Hunt who was the mastermind holding the clipboard.

Teko was elated at the news that Gavin would be joining Matsatsantsa. Gavin turned sloppy players into average ones, and average players into great ones. Imagine what he could do with a player like Teko?

Teko also needed a change from Pitso, because if there's one style of leadership that Teko doesn't respond well to it is demoralisation. 'I'm not lazy, I just don't like being put down. It brings back memories of my family growing up. Painful memories.'

Before the change in coach, Teko got his first Bafana Bafana call-up. It was great for him to be playing in the green and gold, but he wasn't overly excited, mainly because of the sub-standard tournament that he had been called up to play in.

The COSAFA Cup is a regional competition between the southern African sides. The Bafana team selected for 2007 was an extremely experimental one. There were youngsters and misfits everywhere you looked. Teko wanted to play with Benni McCarthy; only then would he really feel like a Bafana player.

Nonetheless, he gave it his all, and he delivered like only Teko could. Incredibly, he scored two goals in his second-ever game for Bafana Bafana. He scored every goal for South Africa on the way to the final and finished the tournament as the competition's top goal scorer. South Africa came home with the gold medal.

Teko may have stolen the show in his first international tournament, but what many don't know is that he had almost not made the flight, and that was because of his lover, Linky.

As Teko slowly became more and more famous, Linky started changing. She wanted things to stay the way they were – nice and simple, just her and Teko. When Teko joined SuperSport United, things started to go wrong between him and Linky.

When Teko received his first national call-up to go and play for Bafana Bafana in May 2007, Linky did the unthinkable. Being a new recruit, Teko had to be impressive; he had to be presentable, display a good attitude and, most importantly, he had to be punctual. This was proving difficult, as Linky decided to hide Teko's passport. A major panic set in Teko's chest. Excuses like a missing passport would not fly with the national team. He knew she had hidden it but she was denying it. Teko started running around the house, flipping furniture and pulling books out of the shelf. He was going crazy; he needed to find his passport. A massive argument ensued.

After that incident, Teko realised that his issues with Linky would only get worse. If she was struggling to live with his fame now, then she would never handle sharing him with the millions of supporters he was to gain when he moved to a big team. Teko realised that if they stayed together, it could become difficult and she might feel resentment and start causing trouble for him.

Teko had ambitions. He wanted to be a superstar. He wanted to be the darling of Bafana Bafana. He wanted to play in the World Cup. He felt as though she was holding him back.

He did not give up on her easily, though. Their relationship had gone on for too long for it to be thrown out overnight like unwanted food. He thought he would try one more time: 'Listen, come to Johannesburg and live with me. Leave Limpopo, come study here in Joburg; I'll pay your fees and we can live in the same house.'

Teko tried and tried because he really wanted a family. However, it was not to be. Linky wanted a simple life and the sunny fields of Limpopo; Teko sought more.

'I regret that things never worked out between us. We were supposed to be together; I just couldn't stay, though. I couldn't stay in Limpopo because of her insecurities. In hindsight, I don't think anything could have worked at my peak.'

Teko is popular with women. He's a charming guy, a talented guy, an intelligent guy, and the money helps too. Sometimes Teko wonders why it is so difficult to find a solid relationship. He looks at a guy like Jabu Mahlangu (formerly Jabu Pule). Through all his troubles, drinking and other bad habits, he has been with the same partner who has stuck with him through the highs and the lows. When Teko looks back upon his lovers, he wishes that Linky had stuck with him like Jabu Mahlangu's wife.

One of the most difficult things about leaving Linky was the break up with her family and leaving the child they had had together behind. 'That is the hardest thing. When you get to that situation, you think more of the family. You know she may have seen it coming because the signs were there, but her family will never see it coming. The worst part is that you try to do the right thing but sometimes by doing the right thing you end up doing the wrong thing. You try stay with her to make things less painful but you end up hurting yourself and her more. It is the most difficult thing, leaving someone.'

After Teko had made peace with Linky and returned from his dream Bafana Bafana debut, he was called to the main office to meet Gavin Hunt.

'Where do you want to play?' Gavin asked Teko, straight to the point as always.

'I see myself as a number 10, coach,' Teko replied.

'Okay, fine,' Gavin said, scratching his chin. 'I'll try you out as a number 10, but I have a problem.' Of course he had a problem. Head coaches always do. 'My problem is that I have too many players who play the same style. A lot of you are identical. You're one of them.'

He was right. There were many in Pretoria playing like Teko. However, although they were similar, none were quite on his level, and, as usual, when a coach was to find a fault with Teko, they would refer to his attitude more than his playing technique.

If Pitso Mosimane attended the old school, Gavin Hunt was the headmaster. Gavin commanded discipline in his boys; he did not understand someone who wore earrings or wore pants lower than his hips.

SuperSport United jetted off to Australia for a pre-season tournament. It was Teko's first intercontinental flight, and it was Gavin's first game in charge of SuperSport United. As has happened before, the South Africans underestimated an opponent from the east and got a healthy thrashing: 4-1, in favour of the Australians. However, Teko won Man of the Match. It is not every day that you see someone on the losing side of a four-goal drubbing receiving the Man of the Match Award.

Everyone made a big fuss about Teko after the game, and that irritated Gavin greatly. Gavin, like most successful coaches, hates losing, and he is truly frightening when his team does not win. This time was no exception. He was fuming at the team's loss and Teko's Man of the Match Award was the cherry on top: 'I don't know what game those guys were watching! Who gives an award like that to someone on the losing side?'

It was nothing personal against Teko. Gavin was just mad. Gavin holds no grudges, and Teko actually likes that about him.

Later that evening, the team attended a gala dinner. Teko overheard something that made him want to leave SuperSport United instantly. He heard one of the owners of the club saying: 'I don't understand players who accept and celebrate a Man of the Match Award even after they have lost.' It was the last thing Teko needed to hear. He felt he was being crucified once again and he was simply sick of it.

He was rooming with Katlego Mashego at the time, so he decided to ask him why it was that he was always being picked on. Teko felt that an issue that had his name attached to it was always blown out of proportion.

'Maybe because of your quality,' Katlego suggested. 'Maybe they want to keep you grounded.'

'No, man,' Teko said, unsatisfied with the answer. 'I'm leaving SuperSport United.'

'You can't leave,' Katlego protested. 'You're a Bafana player now. You must stay. You're an asset.'

'No,' said Teko. 'I'm leaving. I want to play in the Telkom Charity Cup, and that will never happen here at SuperSport United.'

Teko was right. The Telkom Charity Cup was no small deal. It was the supporters' tournament in South Africa, and possibly the biggest day on the footballing calendar. It was a one-day tournament with four teams participating. Two semi-finals would be played in the morning; there would be some spectacle involving sky divers and trumpet bands in between, and then a mighty final in the afternoon, by which time most supporters could not see or walk straight.

Which four teams participated was all up to the supporters, and therefore SuperSport United would never feature. Fans would call in and vote for their team to participate. Kaizer Chiefs and Orlando Pirates would be a guarantee every time. The other two spots would usually go to a team like Mamelodi Sundowns, Moroka Swallows or Bloemfontein Celtic, although it changed often.

The competition has since changed to a dreary affair, a contest between just Chiefs and Pirates that usually ends in a 0-0 draw. However, when the Charity Cup was still in its heyday, there was nothing that could match it. Teko wanted nothing more than to play in the festival. SuperSport United, despite its various successes as a club, has never attracted a massive support base and is therefore unlikely to be included in such a competition.

Teko made his wishes clear, and tensions were running high. Gavin is not the kind of coach who will beg and plead a player to stay. In fact, he seems to quite enjoy having an excuse to kick them out. Gavin told Teko at one point, 'If you want to go, that's cool with me.' He couldn't exactly figure out what kind of player Teko was, but he knew their styles didn't match. Both were fine with him leaving, there was no bad blood.

After the Australia trip, SuperSport United jetted back home and bussed to the hot and dry fields of Limpopo for another pre-season tournament.

Gavin wanted his best players for the final of the tournament so he kept them on the bench and played his second choices in the first game. Teko was one of those second choices playing the curtain-raiser, and he put on a never-before-seen show.

The first-team players watched from the benches with their jaws on the floor as Teko netted in six goals in that first game. Six goals. It is not often a professional player, or any other player for that matter, scores a double hat-trick in one game.

Teko finished the competition as player of the tournament and top goal scorer. He drops his head, chuckles and lets out a whistle as he shakes his head and recalls the tournament: 'Jirra, jirra.' He laughs again. 'The way I killed it that day, it was a problem, I promise you … A lot of people were not happy with how well I was doing.'

Teko was clear in his mind that he wanted to leave SuperSport United. He was also clear that he was ready for the challenge of a big team so he called his agent, Alex Bondarenko, mainly just for formality's sake.

'Hey, man, I want to leave this club. I want to go to a big club. What are you doing about it?'

'No, Teko, I've been speaking to lots of people. I'm making big plans for you, don't worry.'

Teko was sceptical and wondered if this was true. A further complication was that Teko still owed his agent some money from the SuperSport United deal. Teko approached Jazzman Mahlakgane with his problems.

'Go find out from Alex exactly what you owe him,' Jazzman instructed Teko.

Upon returning and telling Jazzman exactly how much he owed the agent, Jazzman wrote a cheque and paid off Teko's debt to his agent. Teko was now under the guidance of Jazzman, who would be the new father figure in Teko's life. It was not long afterwards that Jazzman was on the phone to Orlando Pirates.

When Jazzman first signed Teko, he laid out a simple rule that he applies to all his new players: 'Boeti, I need to meet your family first.'

Teko was understandably hesitant. Jazzman had arranged to meet Teko's mother and sister, but on the day of the meeting Teko pulled one of his famous disappearing acts. He was nowhere to be found. Teko didn't really want his new agent to know about his difficult upbringing. However, Jazzman started asking around and eventually headed off into Zone 7 by himself.

'When I arrived there, it was really an appalling situation, hey, to say the least. The house was dilapidated. It was in really bad shape.'

After the meeting, Jazzman put his big hand on Teko's shoulder and said, 'Okay, my boy, I've met the family. Now let's get to work.'

One Monday, towards the end of 2007, Teko received a call from Jazzman.

'Orlando Pirates want to sign you tomorrow,' Jazzman said, straight to the point.

'But it's Tuesday tomorrow; I'm supposed to go to training with …'

'Teko!' Jazzman interrupted. 'Did you not hear me? I said Orlando Pirates want to sign you tomorrow and you're still telling me about going to training with whoever.'

The next day, Jazzman picked Teko up and they drove out to Parktown where Teko would meet the Iron Duke, Dr Irvin Khoza, a colossal figure in South African football and chairman of Orlando Pirates.

Teko had met an Orlando Pirates legend before, Screamer Tshabalala, but this was different, this was huge. Meeting the Iron Duke in person was pretty much the closest thing you could get to meeting the president, as a footballer.

Irvin sat Teko down in his office and started talking.

'I won't guarantee you game time. I can't guarantee that you will play. The only thing I can guarantee you is that, with your style of play, Orlando Pirates will change your life forever.'

Irvin went on to tell Teko about the importance supporters hold for the club. Jazzman remembers the moment well: 'Irvin was like a prophet. He had a huge picture of Orlando Stadium behind his desk. In the picture, you could just see thousands of Pirates supporters.'

Dr Khoza kept pointing to the picture and then turned to Teko and said, 'A lot of players don't understand, when you play for this team, you are not just playing for yourself, your teammates, or your family. You are playing for the supporters. There are so many people who are going through all kinds of troubles every day. The only brief period of joy they get in their lives, when they can forget about their worries, is when you play football. You may be playing for people who want to commit suicide, but they may reconsider after watching a good football match. Pirates supporters are the most important thing to this club; people work hard to buy a ticket with their small salaries, but they will take that knock to come watch you play.'

Teko was frozen. He had never thought of it like that. Irvin repeated his earlier sentence: 'I guarantee that Pirates will change your life. The big question is, how will you deal with it?'

Teko never knew how big he was about to be, but Irvin did.

'I'm going to sign you today. Don't tell anyone.'

Teko had grown up a Kaizer Chiefs supporter and had always vocalised this. But he had no problems signing for Pirates. 'I grew up a Kaizer Chiefs fan; I grew up supporting Doctor Khumalo's Kaizer Chiefs, but not this time. I was happy to be a Buccaneer.'

When Irvin says you don't tell, you simply don't tell. However, Teko couldn't help but let something out. Upon his return to

SuperSport United the next day, he walked up to two of the other players, Dennis Masina and Katlego Mashego: 'You guys are going to see me; I'm leaving this club.'

'You're not going anywhere,' they replied.

'Don't worry,' Teko said with a chuckle, 'you will see me this weekend. I will be on TV. I will be there with all the supporters, the whole of South Africa. I will be on TV, where there is singing and shouting. I will be with the vuvuzelas.'

Teko left the SuperSport United training that Wednesday without saying anything to Gavin or any of the other players. He got a call from Jazzman when he got home that evening.

'Teko, report for training with Orlando Pirates tomorrow.'

CHAPTER 12

'South Africa needs you, Teko'

That week in 2007, Teko had received a call from Jazzman on Monday, informing him about Pirates' interest in signing him. On Tuesday, he was signed. On Wednesday, he left SuperSport United. On Thursday, he reported for Orlando Pirates training. This was as big as it got in South African football.

There were many players at that first Pirates training session – 50 or 60. The first thing the coaches did was divide the group into two: those who were playing in the Telkom Knockout that weekend, and those who weren't. Teko was in the latter group.

Jabu Mahlangu was there. Jabu had seen it all and done it all. He was a tiny midfield magician whose tricks haunt defenders' memories to this day. His first professional club was Kaizer Chiefs; he was an absolute menace on the ball. No words can do his skill justice. His only problem was that he was naughty, 'Ngwana wa Tshwenya'. He had a love for the bottle, but he's a clean, sober, larger-than-life and fantastic role model for the country now.

One thing about Jabu that never changed was the fact that he was always a phenomenal footballer. Before Teko joined the Pirates, another thing that had never changed was Jabu's shirt number: 11.

Jabu was handed the shirt number 11 at Kaizer Chiefs, a jersey once worn by the magnificent Teenage Dladla and the hypnotising Scara Ngobese. He kept the number-11 jersey at Orlando Pirates.

'South Africa needs you, Teko'

Then, on Teko Modise's first day of training, Jabu arrived and was handed a different number. The Orlando Pirates officials gave Teko the shirt number 11.

That moment really struck Teko. He thought to himself that if Pirates could do that to Jabu, then you know the club is bigger than anyone. People were crazy about Jabu, Teko was a massive fan too, and here he was taking Jabu's shirt. The number 11 was now on Teko's back, and the pressure was on Teko's shoulders.

By Friday, Teko was on the front page of the *Sowetan*. The nation officially knew he was a Buccaneer. The Telkom Charity Cup was on Saturday and Teko was still training in the group that was not meant to be playing.

Game day arrived. When the players arrived at the stadium to warm up for the game, Teko was handed another surprise. He was told that he would in fact be playing. He felt the same nervousness he had felt when he was that kid who over-ate before his debut for Ria Stars.

It was one of the biggest moments of Teko's life. He never truly understood how big you could be as a footballer. The first game was due to take place in the morning, and as fate would have it, Orlando Pirates drew Kaizer Chiefs in the first round.

Teko, like Doctor Khumalo and Jabu Mahlangu, is one of the few players who can claim to have made their debut in a Soweto derby. Teko never anticipated the noise, the pressure, the atmosphere, the passion, the tears, anger and elation. It was such an emotional experience for the supporters and the players. When Kaizer Chiefs and Orlando Pirates play, it feels as if the world stops spinning in Soweto for 90 minutes.

'I learnt more in that one weekend than I have learnt in my whole career up to that point. All my time with SuperSport United, Ria Stars, City Pillars, whatever, it didn't add up to what I experienced that first day. It all came to me in that moment when I realised just how passionate Pirates supporters were. I realised what the team meant and, more importantly, what the badge meant to millions of South Africans. I remember what Irvin Khoza told me when he signed me, and suddenly it all made sense,' Teko recalls.

There was a lot to get used to at Orlando Pirates. One of the most interesting things was the role of muti. The South African football scene is filled with unique traditions and beliefs. Teams will try anything to get an edge over their opponents. Most teams have a sangoma they consult, a spiritual intermediary who will try to ensure victory for the team. When Teko arrived at Pirates, he met their resident sangoma who had been there for a while. In Teko's first week, the sangoma said he was going to try out something new. In the change room before the game, the sangoma placed a stick at the entrance. All the players had to jump back and forth over the stick. Pirates lost that game.

If they lost a game, they would go back to the sangoma and say, 'Hey, wena, your muti is not working. You made us lose!'

'No, relax, next week I will bring different muti and you will see it will work,' the sangoma would protest.

Teko used to say to him, 'Hey, listen, you have been here for long. If the muti you were using last season was working then keep using that muti; why do you want to experiment now? Just use the same muti.'

And so the sangoma would revert to the classic ritual – the bath. The players would be woken up at midnight before a game and made to bath in water mixed with a specially prepared concoction of herbs and other ingredients. Many players were religious and these practices made them uncomfortable. However, at Orlando Pirates everything is performed as a team. Religious or not, you get in the bath.

The players would bath in the special mixture, then shower, climb back into bed and try to sleep before the game. Even with this practice the results on the field were not improving; and the sangoma was under pressure. He determined that the players were not using his muti correctly. He realised that they were showering after their bath and therefore the muti was washed off, so he devised a new plan.

Now, instead of the players bathing at midnight, before the game, they would grab their bags, go bath in the special baths, then get on the bus and go to the stadium.

'The water was very black,' Teko recalls. 'You have no idea what is in there. You could see some sticks and leaves but who knows what else was in there. It would be very itchy, very strange.'

The biggest problem with this ritual was when they had to play at night. As they could not dry off their bodies their players' jerseys would be damp, their socks would be damp and they would become very cold and uncomfortable.

Teko devised a plan to deal with this problem. Before the game, he would secretly take a pair of scissors and cut a hole in his socks at his Achilles heels. He did this to let some air in and dry his socks because, as things stood, he could not feel his feet and it was making him play poorly. The sangoma would even put some substance inside their socks before the team played, so it was itchy and uncomfortable.

When the sangoma found out that Teko had been cutting his socks he was livid. He said that the muti would not work if Teko was cutting his socks. Furthermore, some of the other players started following Teko's lead when it came to relieving the discomfort.

It was such a problem that it escalated to management. The team manager had to pull Teko aside to address the issue.

Teko carefully explained that he respected the traditions of the club but the muti could not come at the price of him playing poorly. If his feet were cold he could not perform well. Management accepted his reasoning; they would have accepted anything from Teko – he started his Pirates career like a petrol tank on fire. His efforts had not gone unnoticed and two weeks after his debut Teko was summoned into Dr Irvin Khoza's daunting office once again.

'You know, Teko,' Irvin said, 'you have the potential to be something truly great at this club. The way you play, you could be something big. You could be bigger than Steve Lekoelea.'

Teko burst out laughing. He knew that the only person bigger than Steve Lekoelea to pass through Orlando Pirates was Jomo Sono.

'I used to watch Steve make people go crazy,' Teko recalls. 'I used to go crazy over Steve. He was something else. I didn't believe Irvin's comparison for one second.'

Irvin urged Teko to be more, to focus more, to be more arrogant about his abilities. Irvin believed that if Teko truly backed himself, there was no limit for the boy.

Those words were all Teko needed to hear. He responded better to compliments than criticisms. This was also not just any compliment; this came from the Iron Duke himself, Dr Irvin Khoza throwing his weight behind Teko. It was a big deal.

Teko started becoming a different player. He adopted a different mentality; his work rate spiked and his attitude adjusted to life in the limelight. He became a pivotal player in the team. He arrived and put some of the established names on the bench. One such man was Joseph 'Duku Duku' Makhanya who played close to 150 games for Orlando Pirates.

One day Duku Duku came to Teko and said: 'I'm not even bitter that you have replaced me and now I'm on the bench. I'm just happy that Pirates finally started signing quality players.'

After Teko's debut for Pirates, things went upwards. Jazzman's phone did not stop ringing; everyone wanted to sign him, endorse him, or offer their daughter to marry him.

In the lead-up to the 2009 Confederations Cup, there was a huge hype about which sportsman should be the next McDonald's ambassador. To put into context how big a deal this is, the previous ambassador was Michael Ballack – one of the top goal scorers in German footballing history, a former Bayern Munich and Chelsea superstar and World Cup finalist. His contract as the McDonald's ambassador was drawing to a close. Jazzman jumped at the opportunity.

McDonald's was already eyeing a number of South African players at the time, including Captain Aaron Mokoena and the internationally renowned Steven Pienaar. Out of the talented pool of players, Teko was named the McDonald's ambassador.

As soon as the endorsement deals started flowing, Jazzman issued a directive to Teko: 'Part of this money from these endorsement deals that you are earning now, I'm taking it and we are fixing your mother's house.'

Jazzman stayed true to his word. He sent a construction

company and landscaping company to Teko's mother's house in Soweto. Jazzman redid the house in the way he knew Teko liked. He orchestrated a garden outside, put in new floor tiles, new kitchen units, new couches and a brand-new TV for his mother.

This all happened at the crest of Teko's career, as he became the heartbeat of Soweto. This was when he started earning his nicknames. Every South African player worth his salt earns a nickname. Some called Teko 'the Navigator' for his guidance and direction as a midfielder; others called him 'Google Earth', for his ability to map the field of play. However, his key nickname is the one that describes him the best: 'the General'.

The General sets the pace, decides the motion; he dictates the flow and controls the game. Nothing happens without his blessing and nothing escapes his eye. The General is ever present; he sets off the wings on their runs and places the ball for the striker to score. The General is the link. He connects the defence to the attack. One wrong move from the General and the whole army crumbles. One right move and victory is almost certain.

Although Teko was playing the best football of his life, and indeed the best football that supporters had seen in a Pirates jersey in a long time, the team wasn't doing particularly well. Orlando Pirates finished eighth, while SuperSport United and Gavin Hunt won their first of three league trophies.

And thus began a rumbling that would plague the player for the rest of his career: The Curse of Teko. It would become a phrase repeated often. The South African footballing world is a particularly superstitious space. Having a curse attached to your name was not a good thing. The Curse of Teko – the best player with the worst luck. He had been one of the best players at SuperSport United, but it took him leaving for them to start winning trophies; the same was playing out for Orlando Pirates. They had the best player in the league but were not in the best position.

For Teko, there was swagger in the soccer, but for his club, there was dust on the trophy cabinet.

Regardless of this, life carried on for Teko and his career kept soaring upwards; things were good, very good. In 2008, Teko played more football games than any other South African. He was in full swing for the national team and Orlando Pirates needed him in almost every minute of every game.

Life started changing for Teko. He bought a bigger house and a more expensive car. He was greeted everywhere he went. He started doing interviews with magazines that had nothing to do with football. White people started asking him for his autograph. Teko Modise was a superstar.

There was one game that truly cemented his reputation. There was a Soweto derby scheduled with a twist: it was due to take place in Durban. This was part of a whole show-and-tell for South Africa as we proudly puffed our feathers in preparation for the 2010 World Cup. The FIFA delegation had arrived to conduct the draw for the World Cup, and while they were here, they decided they wanted to watch a derby.

This derby would also be televised all over the world: Germany, England, America, you name it. The world would watch Teko for the first time. He decided to put on a show. The game was a nail-biting, 2-2, explosive affair, and Teko was breathtakingly awesome.

Everything Teko had learnt up to that point in his life came into play. All the legends he had met, the coaches he had fought with, the administrators who had wronged him, the street footballers, the idols he watched on TV. It all culminated in a beautiful performance from the General.

That game changed everything. He never scored but he was the main attraction, the captain and the engine room. He was the General. He dictated the game and absorbed the pressure. He didn't play like anyone else; he had his own unique style, which was direct but efficient. He could do it all: dribble, pass, cross and shoot. The complete package.

From that day, Teko started looking at football differently. He started driving Orlando Pirates. Not only that, he started thinking more about the game and worked on becoming the most intelligent midfielder in the country.

From there, life was smooth sailing. Teko was enjoying his football; he was scoring many crucial goals for Bafana Bafana and Orlando Pirates. His selection for Bafana Bafana was not consistent at first, though. He was in and out of the team because of a player named Papi Zothwane, who was in his place and exceptionally talented.

In September 2007, South Africa were playing Zambia in an AFCON qualifier in Cape Town. Bafana Bafana needed one goal to progress to the competition. Before the game, the senior players were blasting music and dancing in the change room. Coach Carlos Alberto Parreira was not the biggest fan of that kind of behaviour.

'I hope all these smiles and dancing will not cost us the game. I hope you guys are not getting too cocky,' Carlos warned them.

The game turned out to be an absolute disaster. Before the nation could blink, Bafana Bafana found themselves 3-0 down at home. There was drama when Isaac Chansa, a Zambian player, was given a red card and sent off the field. Chansa started walking slowly to waste time. Benni McCarthy, who could at times be an emotional player, walked up to him, put his arms under Isaac's, picked him up and started marching him off the field like a bouncer ejecting a teenager from a nightclub. This resulted in a mini-brawl between the two. It was hilarious to watch from the stands but it was tense and dramatic on the field.

Papi Zothwane, the player often preferred ahead of Teko, had an absolute shocker that day, a truly terrible game. So, Carlos Alberto Parreira brought on Teko Modise. The game finished 3-1 and Bafana qualified. Teko cemented his place in the senior team.

The pinnacle of Teko's Bafana career was when he got to share a change room with Benni McCarthy. As a young boy in Diepkloof, Teko used to watch Brian Baloyi and Benni McCarthy get their hair done in the hood. They were both doing something extravagant before the 1998 AFCON tournament in Burkina Faso where Bafana Bafana finished second. Benni was young, skinny, and finished the tournament as the top goal scorer.

Both Brian Baloyi and Benni McCarthy were established icons. Now here was Teko sharing a change room with them, with the

South African flag over their hearts. In that time, Benni had gone on to win the UEFA Champions League with José Mourinho and FC Porto. Just being around Benni made Teko think he had made it. 'If Benni could admire me and respect me as a footballer then nothing else mattered.' He also really liked playing with Benni. They both found it easy to feed off each other; they were both intelligent footballers.

Teko was on top of the world. Everything that he had put in was bearing fruit. Recognition of his footballing excellence came at the end of the 2008/2009 season when he became the first player to win the South African Footballer of the Year Award.

It was a fairly controversial award in that it had never been awarded to anyone before. People began to ask some questions: What makes someone the greatest footballer of the year? Why did Teko deserve the first one? As with anything, there were those who had their doubts. Most in South Africa, however, believed that Teko was the rightful holder of the award. Whether he deserved it or not, the truth of the matter was that he had to continue to live up to it.

Teko's main drive was the looming World Cup. He was a Bafana regular but he needed to make sure that he was there on opening day in Soccer City playing against Mexico. Inspiration was not difficult to find. He was inspired by how the world around him was rolling into shape; he was inspired by his circumstances, and by the supporters. His idols were now his colleagues, and that also inspired him greatly.

Steven Pienaar, Benni McCarthy, Matthew Booth and Carlos Alberto Parreira were all pushing him in the right direction:

'Go harder, Teko.'
'Go further, Teko.'
'Be better, Teko.'
'Become great, Teko.'
'South Africa needs you, Teko.'

CHAPTER 13

'The family I never had'

'He was the father I never had.'
That's what Teko recalls about his time with Irvin Khoza at Orlando Pirates.

Irvin used to call Teko to his office often and explain to him the importance of his good performances.

'People look up to you in this team, Teko. The other guys look up to you. Even though it is your first season, the players look to you for inspiration. If you don't play well, they won't play well. If they see that you are finding a game difficult, then they will think it's impossible. If you don't give up, they will never give up.'

This was exactly the kind of talk that Teko needed. Irvin Khoza was respecting him as a footballer, and Irvin was not obliged to respect anyone. He has signed some of the greatest players to ever pass through the country and continent. Irvin always knew the right thing to say to get Teko fired up.

Teko was training harder than ever before and he had incredible mental strength. It felt as if the pinnacle of Teko's career was here.

'This is my chance to be better than Doctor Khumalo, just like I always said I would be.'

This was Teko's opportunity to turn a difficult start in life into a success story. But while Teko may have been willing to move on from his past, his past was not willing to move on from him, just yet. In 2009, his father tried to reach out to him. His intentions may

The Curse of Teko Modise

have been good but his method was dodgy. Teko was contacted by the head offices of SABC 1, asking him for a comment.

'Hey, Teko, there is a man here claiming to be your dad.'

But Teko was having none of it. In his eyes, there was a right and a wrong way to go about things. Taking family matters public was always wrong in Teko's eyes.

'My dad knows where my family stays. If he wants to see me he must organise a meeting with the family. He can't just get hold of me on television now that I am Teko Modise. These were issues we could have solved privately. This is the guy who threw me out on the street like I was nothing and never looked back. Now that I'm famous he wants to be with me. If he did things properly and requested a meeting with me by going through my family then I would probably be friends with him to this day. It would have been nice to have a relationship with my father.'

Teko turned his efforts and love back to his club. The Orlando Pirates badge meant everything to him. Irvin was the father he never had and the supporters were the family he wished he had grown up with. Orlando Pirates supporters are not just any group of humans; their passion is explosive and, at times, dangerous.

The supporters absolutely loved Teko, though; they embraced him and gave him the love of a family. Teko played his heart out for them in his first two seasons with Pirates. He knew this was one group of people he could not disappoint.

One of the Orlando Pirates supporters' nicknames is the Happy People, but don't be fooled ... When Gordon Igesund was the coach, long before Teko arrived, some supporters showed up to a Pirates practice in a kombi. The supporters invaded the training pitch with sticks and sjamboks and shook Gordon up. What is even stranger is that Gordon had won the league with Pirates that season – the supporters just weren't happy with the *style* of football that the club was playing. They truly are a fussy group of supporters that you do not want to anger.

Teko made it his aim to never let the Pirates supporters down. 'Because I grew up knowing what it feels like to be let down, I never wanted to do that to people who loved me, the Pirates faithfuls.'

'The family I never had'

For two seasons, Teko ruled the roost at Orlando Pirates. He was a venomous footballer and the darling of the supporters. The team, however, was still not getting the trophies it deserved, so one day Irvin Khoza called on the services of one of the big guns of football. Not South African football, but global football.

In walked Ruud Krol.

Ruud Krol is as tough as they come. He had been a prolific defender with attacking abilities for the Netherlands. He was central to their 'total football' revolution, a new style of football at the time that called for quick, short passing and aggressive forward movement. Ruud Krol was in the Netherlands squad that collected the silver medal in the 1974 and 1978 World Cups. Interestingly, he is one of four players who have scored both a goal and an own goal in a World Cup.

Teko had never heard of him before.

Ruud arrived while Teko was on duty for Bafana Bafana. He was playing more games than anyone in the country at the time so he was given a couple more rest days than the other Pirates players. He knew there was a new coach coming to Pirates. He was not stressed, though – he believed in his abilities and any coach at the time would have put Teko in the starting line-up of any club.

Ruud Krol's first game in charge was a big one. A cup tie against SuperSport United. Ruud Krol decided to put Teko on the bench for that game and Pirates lost 1-0.

Teko swore and cursed the whole way home. He hated losing. More than that, he hated sitting helplessly watching from the sidelines as his team lost. Teko could not understand why Ruud was not playing him. He was the key player in the team.

He had heard that Ruud had played in two World Cups. 'I expected him to understand, as a former player, why I was training less. But he was behaving like a secretary who just became a coach. I was thinking that Pirates had bought a terrible coach. This guy clearly didn't understand South African football.'

Teko did not hold these feelings inside for too long. He went and confronted Ruud about being left out. They had a good, open and honest conversation and the air was cleared. They agreed to

The Curse of Teko Modise

get along. They even started becoming friends.

After their chat, Teko and Ruud started joking and making bets with each other. Ruud would approach Teko with a sheet of paper on the training ground. The Dutchman would dip his glasses, smile and point, showing Teko his statistics from last season.

'Look at this, look how many runs you made, look at your passes, look at your goals.' Ruud looked up and smiled at Teko, 'I will bet you R10 000 that you won't even score 11 goals this season.'

Teko chuckled at the cocky manager. He had scored nine goals the season before and set up many more that he could have been selfish with and claimed the glory.

'Ag, man, 11 is too easy,' Teko said to Ruud. 'Let's make it 12; give me a bit of a challenge.'

They went toe to toe and ego to ego often. If Teko didn't score on the weekend, Ruud would come to him on Monday and say, 'You see, you can't score. I'm going to save my R10 000, thanks for that, Teko.'

It was just his tactic to push Teko further and harder. Teko recognised that and appreciated it, although sometimes with Ruud Krol the difference between challenging and obstructive became blurred. One day, he moved Teko to play on the wing.

Teko hadn't played wing in years, but Ruud's rationale was that Teko was so famous now that he was being marked out of the game by nervous defenders. Furthermore, all the Pirates players seemed to want to pass to Teko more than anyone else, so it made sense to move him.

Teko adapted and thrived. Pirates were doing well under the new coach and they finished second on the log that season.

Teko's contract was also coming to an end. There were serious offers coming in from serious leagues all around the world. One day, Teko called up Jazzman, 'Boss, let's go. Let's get out of here, I'm ready for the next challenge.'

That phone call was the beginning of a slow decay in the relationship between Teko Modise and his beloved Orlando Pirates.

CHAPTER 14

The move that wasn't

Teko knew it was time to leave Orlando Pirates. However, he was very mindful of everything the club had given him. Most importantly, it had given him a popularity he had never known before. It was because of this that he attained personal lucrative sponsorships with big companies such as McDonald's.

At the back of Teko's mind, he knew it was not right just to use Pirates and then dump them. He wanted to make sure that they also benefitted from him going overseas, considering all they had given him. In football, there is only one way to do that, and that is by signing another contract with the team.

If your contract has come to an end, any other club can essentially get you for free. However, if you still have a contract with a team, then any other club that wants your services must pay your current club in accordance with a buy-out clause.

There were many emails going back and forth between Orlando Pirates, Jazzman and various clubs that wanted Teko. Jazzman was cc-ing Teko in all the mails. He could see the figures; he could see the details; he could feel the cold air of Europe, hear the roar of the crowds and see the foreign jersey with 'Modise 10' on the back.

'As a child growing up in Soweto, you wish to play in the PSL. From the PSL, you wish to play for one of the bigger teams in the league. After that, you dream of playing for Bafana Bafana. The only place to go from there is overseas. That is the dream of any young boy from Soweto,' says Teko.

Teko had always been open and honest with Pirates about his ambitions. He told them his childhood dreams; it was up to them to help him achieve these. He told all the people who needed to be told within the club structures, but the news was not taken well by everyone.

Some of the higher-up officials within Pirates took Teko's request to leave as a sign of disrespect. They saw him as selfish and no longer committed to the team. That wasn't the case at all; it was just that his ambitions had outgrown his boots here on South African soil.

He told Pirates that there was no other South African side he wished to play for. He even offered for a clause to be put in the contract stating that, should he fail overseas, he would come back and proudly don the white-and-black jersey of Pirates again.

'Just let me go, though,' Teko pleaded. 'Let me have my dream.' All he wanted was the opportunity.

The process got complicated, with much bickering and fighting. Teko was privy to less and less information. He wanted to speak to Irvin. The Iron Duke would surely understand. But he was told daily, 'The chairman is not around. The chairman is busy; the chairman cannot see you.'

There is no doubt that Irvin was in fact busy. The World Cup was approaching and Irvin was a key role player in organising the successful hosting of the world's biggest multi-country event. This, however, did not help Teko much. The whole thing was demoralising for him. He saw Irvin as the father he never had and, once again, his father had no time for him.

Even Ruud Krol was puzzled about Teko's situation. 'What are you still doing here?' Ruud used to ask him. 'Shouldn't you be overseas?'

'Ja, coach, I'm leaving this season.'

'Okay, but before you go, Teko, you must score me my 12 goals.'

Teko only managed to score 11 that season, so he lost the bet.

However, that was minor. The major issue was that the overseas deal was looking less likely. The first offers that came through were from a number of big clubs in Greece. Initially, Pirates told Teko that they were not willing to release him to Greece because it was not a 'serious footballing country'. They told Teko that they would happily release him elsewhere, just not Greece. Pirates initially appeared to be concerned about Teko's footballing future. As offers began coming in from different countries, it seemed as though Pirates were not willing to release Teko to any other club or country at all. That realisation was earth-shattering for Teko. He went home and thought about how his dream had been crushed. This move would be the one thing that would change his and his family's lives forever, and he felt as though it was being denied him.

Things got petty from there. Teko was called into a disciplinary hearing by the Pirates board later that season. Floyd Mbele, the administrative director, and Screamer Tshabalala, the technical director, were chairing the meeting,

'What's this whole disciplinary hearing about?' Teko asked.

'Your socks,' Screamer replied.

'My socks?'

'Yes, your socks. You were wearing Nike socks and we are sponsored by Adidas.'

'Socks! Really? Is that really what this is about?'

Teko was furious. He had had a personal sponsorship with Nike before arriving at Pirates and had been given special clearance to wear the socks. However, this issue was not the real problem.

'Guys, I just wanna go,' Teko pleaded with them. 'I understand the socks, this and that, whatever, just let me go. I'm not asking anything else, just let me go overseas, give me my clearance.'

'Where do you wanna go?' they asked him.

'Panathinaikos, Middlesbrough FC, those clubs want me. I can make it there.'

Teko was firing up to go. Benni McCarthy had been telling him how great the European leagues were. In Teko's mind, he was already there.

The pleading was pointless. He was told that there was no buy-out clause in his contract, that he must sign with Pirates for a further two years so all the parties involved could make some money. He signed, but his overseas move never happened.

'To be honest with you, that killed me as a footballer. And it killed me even more as a person. It really killed me.'

Teko got on with the job. He carried on going to training, but it was never the same. He had lost his ambition. He stopped listening to any advice Ruud Krol had for him. He began regretting all the blood, sweat and heartache he had sacrificed for Orlando Pirates.

At the height of his career, he was playing football more than anyone in the country. On the Wednesday, he would play for Bafana Bafana against Cameroon and score two goals. On the Saturday, he would play for Orlando Pirates in the same stadium and score two goals again. He gave it his all.

The situation began to affect him on a personal level. His relationship with his soon-to-be wife began to take real strain.

His anger issues followed him to training and then back home again in the afternoon.

He began a harmful ritual. He didn't enjoy his time on the field and he didn't enjoy his time at home. So, every day, after training, he would call his friends over; they would move his three cars out of the garage, move in to the garage themselves, and sit and drink all day.

The one thing Teko has managed to avoid for his entire career, however, is drugs. 'I've never messed with drugs, even though I have been in dark spaces in my life and I have been offered everything for free. I had all kinds of people from all walks of life come up and offer me all kinds of drugs and other solutions to my sadness. I don't know why but the one thing I knew to never mess with was drugs. Plenty people have offered me drugs. I don't know which ones are which; to me drugs are drugs. Even when I used to go to the night clubs, I never even touched one drug. I've just always been this guy that's scared to do things out of my comfort zone. Even weed – it scares the life out of me. I don't know what it will do. I think when I was in that dark space, if I tried anything

I would have become addicted to that. I was, however, buying booze and drinking every single day, because I was so unhappy inside and things weren't working out with Orlando Pirates.'

It was not a secret. Orlando Pirates knew how he felt. And the unhappiness spilled over into the media. Teko never said anything about the situation but there were many reports coming from within the club that Teko had gone AWOL. This was not true.

A rumour was even started among the players that Teko was having an affair with one of the other players' wives. The players tried to contact *Soccer Laduma* to get them to run a story about it, to increase the chances of pressuring Teko out of the club. Luckily, a considerate editor of the paper refused to run the story on the basis that it would be more embarrassing for the other player than for Teko.

Even though Teko was good friends with the player they'd accused Teko of betraying, their friendship never fully recovered after the scandal.

Things were getting more difficult for Teko at Orlando Pirates. There was one game that served as the final straw for Teko. Pirates were set to play Maritzburg United at the Harry Gwala Stadium in KwaZulu-Natal, a hostile battleground at the best of times.

The game was on a Wednesday in November 2010 and the Soweto derby was scheduled for that weekend. Pirates ended up losing the game to Maritzburg United.

When the plane returned from KwaZulu-Natal, Teko called a mate to fetch him. Usually the team bus picks up the players from the airport and takes them to their cars at the Orlando Pirates head office. Then they return the next day to prepare for the next game.

On the way home, Teko phoned Jazzman. 'Jazz, I don't want to play for Orlando Pirates any more. I didn't go to training today, and I'm not going to camp to report for duty tomorrow.'

CHAPTER 15

The number 10 that wasn't

The media had caught on to the fact that Teko went home by himself after the game against Maritzburg United. Rumours started flying. The most talked-about issue in the media was whether Teko would play in the Soweto derby or not. He was the biggest drawcard for the derby in those days; not having Teko was bad for business.

Teko's stay-away did not last very long before he got a call from Irvin Khoza who told him in no uncertain terms that he needed to stop all the nonsense and get back to training the next day at three o'clock at Orlando Stadium.

To his confusion, the following day as he was on his way to training he received a call from Jazzman: 'Teko, they said it's fine, you don't have to go to training today.'

Teko turned around, stopped by the bottle store, bought booze, went home, sat back and drank. It was not as if he had anyone to cry to, so he found comfort in the bottle. He watched the Soweto derby on television the next day from home.

The media rumour mill opened their doors and windows wider; they all theorised about Teko's behaviour and about why he had gone AWOL. To Teko it seemed as if the only way the media could have got certain information was from a source within the team, which made Teko wonder why the team was not keeping the fight internal and choosing instead to air the issues in public.

The number 10 that wasn't

The media was going crazy and wouldn't let the story go; Teko was growing frustrated and suspicious. He wasn't even sure if Jazzman was on his side any more. He didn't know who to believe or what to do. The people who were the most confused, however, were the supporters. The Teko issue was a very emotional one for them; they thought he no longer loved and respected them. No matter who the player is, the supporters will always side with the club in situations like these.

Orlando Pirates tried patching things up. They called Teko in and told him, 'We are considering bringing the number-10 jersey out of retirement for you.'

To understand why this is a big deal, you need to understand what a retired jersey is. There are three retired jerseys at Orlando Pirates, the number 22, the number 1 and the number 10.

A retired jersey means that nobody can wear that number at the club as a mark of respect for a player whose number it was in the past. The number-22 jersey belonged to a dynamite youngster from Limpopo named Lesley Manyathela. He had been a deadly striker, nicknamed Slow Poison. If his early showings were anything to go by, he looked destined to be the greatest striker this country had ever seen. Lesley was only 22 years old when his car flipped on the highway while driving back to Limpopo after an Orlando Pirates game against Jomo Cosmos. He was on his way to visit his mother for Women's Day.

The number-1 jersey was that of Senzo Meyiwa – the Bafana Bafana and Orlando Pirates goalkeeper and captain who was shot and killed at his girlfriend's house in Soweto in 2014.

The last retired jersey is the number 10. That belonged to the great Jomo Sono. Jomo made his debut for Orlando Pirates when he was a young boy watching a Pirates game; they were short a player so roped Jomo in.

There is no shortage of stories about the greatness of Jomo Sono and what he did for Orlando Pirates. One of them holds that he ran out of his wedding early after hearing that Orlando Pirates were losing a match. He changed from his tuxedo into his kit and won the game.

Jomo managed to create three goals and score one to drive Orlando Pirates to win the game 4-2 to a standing ovation from 50 000 supporters.

Orlando Pirates retired the jersey number 10 because they said there would never be a player greater than Jomo wearing that number. Irvin Khoza thought that it was inconceivable for a player of Jomo's talent to ever be seen again. And here they were, offering the jersey to Teko Modise.

Teko appeared to have found his second wind; he was inspired to regain his former greatness. The Confederations Cup, the curtain-raiser to the World Cup, was approaching. On top of that, the thought of wearing the number-10 jersey at Orlando Pirates lit a fire inside of the General.

Let me be the new number 10, Teko thought to himself. Jomo Sono was the old number 10. Let me redefine it, let me be the new number 10, the new Jomo Sono.

Teko went back and put in more effort in training. The drama came, went and came again, much like his place in the starting line-up. Some days he was on the field, some days he was on the bench, but the important thing was that he was slowly becoming himself again.

Unfortunately, this enthusiasm did not last too long. For whatever reason, it became apparent that the number-10 jersey was not about to be handed to him. Teko felt he was, once again, being treated unfairly. And he did what was becoming his usual way of coping with disappointment; he resumed drinking.

He would still go to training but he was hungover and handicapped. In his mind he was truly only happy when he was playing for Bafana Bafana. He would give his all for the nation. He was scoring goals against Canada, goals against Cameroon, goals against Colombia. It felt like he was the nation's hero but the Pirates' villain.

At Pirates, because of his behaviour, Teko was embarrassingly forced to train behind the goalposts, at a distance from his colleagues. His frustration was growing and after being so embarrassed he made up an excuse that someone had broken into his house and he needed to console his family. He went home that day and thought of all the ways he could waste the time away until his contract came to an end. Unable to manage his feelings, he believed he needed to get out of Pirates as soon as he could. At least for now he had the national team to draw joy from.

Teko's body was in fantastic shape, but his mind was not at ease. He had more problems than any footballer can take on and still be effective on the field. There was still a distant glimmer of hope that his move overseas would miraculously materialise, but after the Confederations Cup, it became clear that his dream was over.

Irvin Khoza had arranged to meet Jazzman over the issue.

'I heard there are some clubs looking for Teko. Which clubs are these?'

'There are a few of them; there is West Bromwich and Southampton from England and a number of teams from Greece.'

Dr Irvin Khoza was in a tricky position. Not only was he the chairman of Orlando Pirates, but he was also head of the organising committee for the upcoming World Cup. Teko was the Iron Duke's player at both a national and club level. So, Irvin Khoza came up with a suggestion: 'Listen, Jazzman, the World Cup is coming soon. It might not be a good idea for that boy to go to Greece or anywhere else. Let him focus. He is our big star. Let's get the World Cup over and done with and then afterwards we can see what happens ...'

But for Teko at the time, in his mind, he was already overseas. He was not interested in hanging around for what felt like the sake of convenience.

Jazzman's phone still did not stop ringing. Spanish side Osasuna now wanted to sign Teko, without even having him over for a trial. Jazzman could see Teko slowly losing his enthusiasm. He could see the deals slipping away and that was killing Teko.

Jazzman had to be there for Teko. He tried to keep him grounded. The unfortunate thing about holding such superstar status is that everyone offers a word in your ear. It seemed that everyone was talking to Teko at once, giving him advice (both helpful and not), offering him things, telling him things.

Confused and uncertain at some point, Teko did not even know where Jazzman stood in his life. In the mix of so many people giving him advice, it became more difficult to tell one voice from the other. Jazzman decided to wait and take a backseat. He could not advise Teko any more; he just had to manage the situation and try to make sure that nothing went too far wrong.

At some point, Teko and Jazzman had such a big fight that they did not speak for two months. Teko blocked Jazzman's number. Teko was nowhere to be found, which made life incredibly difficult for Jazzman, who was trying to organise a move for Teko, away from Orlando Pirates. Eventually, Teko got hold of Jazzman.

'Listen, Teko, we have to face reality. The overseas move is not happening. We need to make a different plan, and Mamelodi Sundowns is busy talking to Pirates about bringing you over.'

Times were dark and Teko needed a release. Like many unable to deal with the hurt of their circumstances, he wanted physical pain to match the pain he felt in his mind and heart. At first glance, you may not notice all of Teko's ink. There is much more that grabs your eye before that. Initially, you will notice his slender build, his superstar status, and his swaggered appearance. However, if you get to stand close enough to him you will notice two hands clasped in prayer on his neck. If you look at his arms, you will see stars, devils and brick walls. Most of Teko's tattoos came about when he was going through a dip in form with Orlando Pirates and it was becoming even clearer that his overseas move was being sabotaged.

'I was so used to pain at that point in my life. There was pain around every corner. I eventually got to a stage where I just wanted more pain.'

Tattoos are painful. The needle is relentless as it rips through the skin of its victim. The process is slow and ruthless, and it is impossible to become used to the pain. For Teko, a tattoo is particularly painful. Because of his skinny build, anywhere the needle cut through his skin, it would go straight to his bone. In his dark days, his first tattoo was a tiger on his chest.

'I just felt like I was so alone at the time. I felt like I was in the jungle, like I was hunting. I did not feel like a king though, so I did not get a lion. I felt like I was playing my heart out for my club and getting nothing in return. So, I got a big tiger tattooed to my chest. It was crazy how painful it was. I almost didn't finish it because it was so painful.' After the tiger was completed. Teko began working on his full sleeves – the entire arm tattooed from shoulder to hand.

Teko had two arms to work with as canvases. He also reasoned that there are two sides to every story: true and false, good and evil, white and black, left and right. He wanted each arm to represent the contrasting fortunes in his life: 'Everyone is capable of both good and evil.'

Teko reasoned that he had been good for so long and tried to do the right thing without any reward that now perhaps he could be bad.

Teko wanted his full sleeves to be freehand. He wanted as little planning and design as possible. He had a friend who was a tattoo artist in Soweto. This friend would come over for hours at a time on Sundays when Teko was not working. They would relax, smoke hubbly, speak a little about what Teko wanted done and then the tattoo artist would get to work.

On Teko's right shoulder, he has a rosary. Many of Teko's tattoos are meant to represent his relationship with God – a complicated relationship, one that he does not often speak about, but at a basic level, he is a Christian believer, a person who prays, and a churchgoer. Also on Teko's right arm is a collection of stars, some clouds and other symbols representing the earth. At the point where his bicep joins his forearm, he has a brick wall, a very large brick wall. Many people confuse the square brick shapes with the classic Louis Vuitton pattern, because of Teko's love for that fashion label.

The brick wall represents a barrier, a mental barrier that he could not break through. His difficulties seemed indomitable, a wall that was too high to climb over, too deep to crawl under and too strong to break through.

Teko's left arm largely illustrates the evil forces in life and many of the challenges he has faced along the way. On this arm is a small, dancing red devil sadistically holding a pitchfork, and these images are most symbolic of the pain he was feeling at that time.

'At the time, I thought that even if I had to die right there and then, nobody would care. I thought that even if I had to do something really bad like take drugs, nobody would care because it would have been expected of me.'

Teko has a tattoo on his back. It is a quote that refers to God protecting him from his enemies. He got it at a time when the supporters of Orlando Pirates were breathing down his neck and he felt as though he needed the protection.

Teko also has a tattoo on either side of his neck, although he is wary of taking these kinds of tattoos too far.

'I didn't want too much ink on my neck because I know one day I'm going to have to put down my boots and pick up a suit and tie,' Teko says with a chuckle.

But now the time had come and the newly tattooed Teko Modise had to put his club and home troubles behind him. South Africa needed him. The Confederations Cup was looming. It was time to focus on the nation.

CHAPTER 16
Joel Santana

If you don't know who Joel Santana is, it is a simple story. After it was announced that South Africa would be hosting the 2010 FIFA World Cup, the powers that be decided that the country needed a proper coach, a real coach, a professional coach – a Brazilian coach.

In walked Carlos Alberto Parreira, a master tactician who had won the World Cup previously with Brazil in 1994. He brought fantastic attacking discipline to our players, hope to our nation and a deficit to our bank balance. It cost roughly R1 million a month to employ him. Unfortunately, though, in 2008, he had to abandon his post, as he needed to return home to tend to his wife, who had fallen ill. Luckily, though, Parreira had a solution.

He suggested that his Brazilian buddy, Joel Santana, take over the job, on the condition that Santana would be earning the same million-a-month salary as Parreira. Santana was everything Parreira was not. In fact, the only thing they had in common was that they were both Brazilian. Santana had coached just about every club team in Brazil and the Middle East, but he had never coached a national team.

The best part about Joel Santana?

He could barely speak a word of English, and seeing as South African footballers are not known for their grasp of the Portuguese language, there were many challenges to his appointment. His post-match interviews were about as close as you could get to a footballing stand-up comedian. In hindsight, it is widely regarded that in Santana, Brazil had sold us a lemon wrapped in tinfoil promising to be a T-bone steak.

We can laugh about it now, but at the time it was far from funny. At first it took the players a long time to adapt to his system of play. They found him so defensive in his approach that it made them uncomfortable.

Teko recalls Santana fondly. He liked him, and what he remembers most about Santana is his character. In stark contrast to Carlos Alberto Parreira, who was reserved and observant, Santana was funny, loud and excitable.

Joel Santana liked Teko a lot. SAFA, the football association, had put Santana up in a hotel room in Sandton. Outside his hotel room was a giant billboard overlooking the highway and it had Teko's name and face on it. He had heard about Teko – people had told Santana what Teko meant to the national team, as well as to the country in general. He struggled with pronunciation though, so he used to say 'Modise' as 'Mogeshi'.

'Hey, Mogeshi, I see you every day there by my hotel. You are there right by my window! You are the billboard!' He used to make a joke about the billboard every day. Every. Single. Day. 'Mogeshi! Do you live in Sandton? Do you live in the big billboard?'

In the lead-up to the World Cup, the football association decided that the South African players were not physical or tough enough and that they had to tour Europe to be knocked around a bit. The first stop was Norway; Bafana Bafana lost. The second stop was Iceland; Bafana Bafana lost again. Santana spent most of his time screaming at the referee, except he never called them 'ref' as is the custom. He used to call them 'Mr FIFA'.

The Iceland game in particular was a disaster. South Africa, with a population of 56 million people, had lost to a country with a population of just over three hundred thousand. South Africa's prospects for the World Cup looked bleak, but Santanas's post-match interview was a thing of comical beauty:

'No, I think is good game. Play well. Score well. Good South

Africa. We look good, it's very good!'

It appeared as if no one had told Santana that we had in fact lost the game.

The players loved Joel Santana, though; they loved his jokes, 'even if he was not really joking per se', Teko recalls with a smile.

Footballers hate team meetings. They hate video sessions and tactical meetings, Teko especially. All he wants is a football at his feet and the sun on his back. There is only one time in Teko's life that he enjoyed team meetings, and that was when Joel Santana was the Bafana Bafana coach.

'Footballers, wow, we hate team meetings. We can't concentrate. But with Joel Santana …' Teko pauses to shake his head and laugh as he recalls the Brazilian. 'We used to look forward to meetings, we used to rub our hands and lick our lips. We knew with Santana it was gonna be comedy. We knew we would be in store for something to laugh about for the rest of the day.'

Santana used to start his speeches in Portuguese, and his assistant would translate for him. This used to disappoint the players. They didn't want him speaking Portuguese; they wanted to him to try his hand at English.

He would get there eventually, though; once he got warmed up, he would get into English.

'We loved it once he got comfortable enough to speak English. We would laugh and laugh the whole day.'

Santana used to enjoy the fact that he made the players laugh, but he used to get very worked up really quickly. There was one player who got under his skin more than any other, a right-footed defender named Bryce Moon.

Bryce was a joker – he was constantly doing something to make the players laugh at practice. In the lead-up to the Confederations Cup, a crew of cameramen had shown up at practice to film Bafana Bafana in preparation for their next game. Santana didn't want them to figure out or record his starting XI, so he changed the team around and confused everyone, including the players. Bryce did something, a little practical joke, and it caused the whole team to stop and laugh.

The Curse of Teko Modise

Santana lost his cool in front of the cameras. He started shouting, screaming and stomping his feet. One of Santana's defining features was that he used to wear sunglasses all the time, even if it was rainy and cloudy. As he was standing on the training ground shouting at Bryce Moon, he took his sunglasses off his face and threw them on the ground. His voice got higher and the line between Portuguese and English was becoming more blurred. Next, he took his play book and threw it on the ground. He was furious and shouting; the players had no idea what he was saying. Bryce was trying to keep a straight face. The cameras naturally tilted their tripods away from the players towards the screaming Brazilian. There was never a dull moment with Santana.

The cameras were watching closely the whole time, because it was a pressured time with the Confederations Cup soon approaching. Bafana Bafana would be up against the champions of all five continents.

Bryce Moon's tournament ended in tragedy; leaving a party after Bafana's last game, he drove into a 25-year-old woman, Mavis Ncube, killing her. He was found guilty of culpable homicide, but acquitted of murder, attempted murder, and drunk and reckless driving.

But before the tragic accident and in the build-up to the tournament, Bafana Bafana were trying to test themselves against similar opponents to those they would be facing in the World Cup. They were set to play Chile during this time. That night in camp, Joel Santana refused to eat dinner. When asked why he was not eating he said, 'No, I don't need to eat. I will be eating chillies tomorrow!' No one in the team had really heard about Alexis Sánchez from Chile before. If Santana had heard of him, he probably would have eaten dinner the night before …

Teko recalls the game against Chile as one of the toughest that he ever played for Bafana Bafana. Chile ran circles around South Africa and Sánchez was the master puppeteer pulling the strings. This was before he became an Arsenal superstar, but on that night in South Africa, he showed that he was well on his way to something great. Chile won the game 2-0.

The jury is still out on Joel Santana and what he did or didn't do for South African football. Like any coach, he had his good moments as well as the bad. However, if there was a time when his 'master plan' came together in a respectable way, it was during the 2009 Confederations Cup.

The Confederations Cup is a competition that serves as a 'practice run' for the World Cup. It happens in the host country a year before the World Cup and the champions of Europe, North America, South America, Asia, Australasia and Africa compete in it, as well as the previous World Cup Champions – in this case, Italy.

South Africa exceeded expectations in both hosting and playing. In the opening game, South Africa played Iraq, the Asian champions. It was a grinding affair, but Teko won the Man of the Match with a fantastic display in midfield. Bafana Bafana would go on to beat New Zealand 2-0 and then lose 2-0 to Spain.

South Africa qualified for the next round, where they were due to play Brazil. That is one game that made people believe. That was one game that made people sit up and take South Africa seriously as a footballing nation. Bafana Bafana tend to up their game against big opposition and, on that night, it was no different. It was difficult to tell which team was the footballing powerhouse.

Teko recalls that Santana was obsessed with beating Brazil. They prepared for that game like it was the World Cup Final. If you watch the highlights package, it is mainly a collection of vicious attacks by South Africa on the Brazilian goal, and images of Kaká with his hands clasped about his head, wondering if they were going to make it out of the game alive. But Bafana Bafana just couldn't find the back of the net, and then, in the 88th minute, Dani Alves of Brazil slotted home a demonic free kick. Its power was such that you could hear 56 million hearts shattering as the ball hit the back of the net.

South Africa exited in the semi-final, but they walked out with their heads held high. After the game, German footballing legend Franz Beckenbauer said that if South Africa could find a goal scorer, they could be considered one of the favourites to win the World Cup.

In the other semi-final, Spain surprisingly lost out to the USA, meaning that South Africa would battle Spain in the third/fourth place playoff. Bafana Bafana vs Spain is always an explosive affair and this time was no different.

The game was stuck at 2-1 in favour of Spain. It was the last minute of the match and South Africa were awarded a free kick from an impossible 30 metres away from the goal. The commentator leaned forward and whispered into his microphone, 'This is South Africa's last hope of taking the game into extra time.'

South African striker Katlego Mphela placed the ball down gently and took a few steps backwards before looking to the goal in the distance, with iconic goalkeeper Iker Casillas standing firm with his hands ready.

'South Africa's last hope,' the commentator repeated as Mphela took a few steps back to prepare for the strike, 'and it requires something very, very spectacular … Like that!' The commentator screamed. He could hardly believe his eyes and neither could the nation. Mphela had done the impossible: he slammed a free kick into the top-right corner, out of the reach of the best goalkeeper in the world.

The goal was an instant classic, one of the best in the world. It earned Mphela a nomination for the Puskás Award, an accolade for the best goal in the world for the year.

South Africa managed to push the game into extra time, but, as the story goes, every triumph is followed by its ugly sister, heartbreak. Spain scored in extra time to win the game 3-2.

South Africa were out but not down: it was a respectable performance against the best in the world. Santana had steered the ship through rough waters, but it would not be long before he was made to walk the plank. There was an old captain back in town. Carlos Alberto Parreira decided he was ready, once again, to lead Bafana Bafana in the World Cup.

Joel Santana, hilarious as he was, was actually not funny enough to distract the country from his poor results. Under Joel Santana, Bafana Bafana lost eight of their nine games in the lead-up to the tournament. The World Cup was approaching and we had to assemble a respectable football team.

Joel Santana would go on to star in a number of television commercials, which made fun of his poor English. It turned out that his post-match interviews were somewhat of a craze in his native land and so Joel Santana, the specialist at making money in unusual ways and confusing a lot of people in the process, carried on doing what he did best.

CHAPTER 17

The World Cup

In the build-up to the World Cup, Bafana Bafana prepared very well. Parreira took them to a camp in Brazil and then another one in Germany. Away from all the hype, glitz and glamour, the boys could just enjoy their game, and they were looking good and playing well.

Spending so much time outside of South Africa helped Teko. He was, for that time, free of the billboards, radio adverts and television commercials all chanting his name and praising him as a hero. He was relaxed and played his football with joy, just like when he was a kid.

Upon return from these camps, the pressure was immense. The whole country was gripped in the hysteria of the 2010 World Cup. It was the biggest thing to hit South African shores since democracy. Every house had a South African flag hoisted above the garage; people put the flag on their car side-view mirrors. Teko Modise's face was everywhere. He was our ace in the pack, our own home-grown Andrés Iniesta. He was on billboards, posters, television and radio. He was our hope.

Before the tournament, a parade was organised. Bafana Bafana drove around Sandton and other upmarket areas in Gauteng as millions of fans painted the streets yellow and cheered our boys on. It was a massive spectacle. This bus parade confused coach Carlos Alberto Parreira, who noted that he had never been in a parade *before* a team had won a trophy.

This didn't help the boys in their quest to deal with the pressure. They were, by all accounts, the mice in a lion's den. Up against the greats: Thierry Henry, Patrice Evra, Franck Ribéry, Giovani dos Santos, Javier Hernández, Diego Forlán, Luis Suárez. A slaughter was expected.

On 11 June 2010 in Soweto, the tunnel was shaking. The floor beneath their boots was pulsating. It felt as if the walls were closing in. It was dark in there. Darkness was everywhere, in fact. The only light to be spotted was dead ahead of them. The noise was paralysing. The war drums were beating and the trumpets echoed in their ears. The noise, sights and smells – those things were pretty tangible. But the most tangible thing was the atmosphere; it seemed to become a physical pressure that squeezed the chests and backs of the men. It was tremendous, magnificent and daunting.

It was here. Ke nako.

FNB Stadium, known during the World Cup as Soccer City, had never witnessed a day as big as this one. The noise and movement coming from outside the tunnel were so overpowering that it made the studs vibrate beneath the players' boots.

Teko looked forward. This was the moment he had been waiting for. A Bafana Bafana team had never played before a crowd this size on home soil in the entire history of the country. The emotions felt by Teko in that moment are indescribable. This was everything he had worked for his whole life. This was everything he had suffered for. From eating out of dustbins, to playing in the bumpy fields of Limpopo, to the fame and bright lights of Orlando Pirates, he had arrived at this. Standing in the tunnel of Soccer City, preparing to take the field for the opening game of the FIFA World Cup; this is as big as it gets for any footballer anywhere in the world.

Alongside him were men from similar backgrounds. A few steps behind in the line was Reneilwe 'Yeye' Letsholonyane. As you will remember, Teko and Yeye first met at trials in a tournament in Soweto at the age of 15. They were just naughty boys then, kicking around for the fun of it and using football as a distraction from poverty, but here they stood, with the South African flag over their hearts, preparing to kick off the biggest sporting event in the world. They were no longer those young boys. No, they were the giants of the country, icons, colossal figures. Now there were 15-year-old boys in Soweto on a field somewhere saying, 'One day I want to be as good as Teko. I want to play like Yeye.'

They walked out onto the field. The noise was paralysing once again. Teko took it one step at a time as they filed into line and waited for the national anthem. The ground was blessed.

The game itself lived up to expectations. Thousands of people, most of them wearing the yellow colours of South Africa and blasting their vuvuzelas, were treated to a spectacle.

It was a gruelling, nail-biting encounter. Mexico were all over South Africa; they had many close-call chances but luckily, thanks to the South African goalkeeping superhero Itumeleng Khune, Bafana stayed in the game.

There is one image that no South African will forget from that day: Siphiwe Tshabalala, with his body distorted, both feet in the air, fists clenched and face crinkled as he fired the shot of his life. It was the 55th minute. Tshabalala received the ball on the left side of the box; he took one touch to control the ball. He was very far left in the box so the angle was tight, but he fired anyway. The shot was a rocket, a screamer, a scorcher, a banger, a thunderbolt. It was spectacular, smashing through the roof of the net. The nation was in a state of collective wonder. That goal earned Siphiwe Tshabalala a nomination for the Puskás Award, given to the global goal of the year, the same award that Katlego Mphela had been nominated for the previous year for his stunner against Spain.

The happiness from Tshabalala's goal did not last long. The rest of the game, and the rest of the tournament, served as a good metaphor for Bafana Bafana in general – so close yet so far. Mexico equalised and we hit the post. A game that should have been ours just wasn't to be. It was a tough tournament for the hosts. The World Cup is a different stage all together, and sometimes it feels less like sport and more like a full-on war between nations.

Bafana Bafana were the seeded team, meaning that they were placed first in a group so that none of the other heavyweights could get drawn in the same group and this didn't quite work out too well.

Alongside Bafana Bafana were Mexico, France and Uruguay. All footballing powerhouses in their own right. We were the only group with two previous World Cup champions in it. Interestingly, the first-ever World Cup game was played between France and Uruguay in 1930. France won 4-1 but Uruguay ended up winning the tournament.

After holding their own against Mexico, Bafana Bafana had a disastrous match against Uruguay. 'Uruguay was the most dangerous when we were in possession of the ball. They pressed us and made it difficult for us to work,' Teko recalls.

In the game, superstar Itumeleng Khune got a red card for a foul against Luis Suárez. This made Khune only the second-ever goalkeeper in the history of the World Cup to receive a red card. As a result, South Africa lost the game 3-0. It was a heart-breaking humiliation at the Loftus Versfeld Stadium in Pretoria.

Bafana needn't feel too bad, though. Uruguay was a quality team and they went on to the semi-finals of the competition. Uruguay were facing Ghana in the quarter-finals. An African team had never made it to the semi-finals of a World Cup before, and it looked like Ghana would be the first. The game was tied up at 1-1. In the final minute of the game, Ghanaian Stephen Appiah headed the ball into the empty Uruguayan net and it was as good as in. Done and dusted. Game. Set. Match. Africa would have their first-ever World Cup semi-final. But as the ball was a centimetre from crossing the line, Luis Suárez stuck his hand up and slapped the ball out of the goal. The referee gave Ghana a penalty and Suárez a red card. Asamoah Gyan stepped up to take the penalty and hit the cross bar. Luis Suárez celebrated Ghana's miss. The game went on to a penalty shootout and Ghana lost. Luis Suárez had robbed Africa of a semi-final place, becoming the most hated man on the face of the continent. To quote the words of South African radio presenter Jeremy Mansfield: 'Luis Suárez, you bastard.'

That was later in the tournament, though. For now, Bafana Bafana had to focus on their last remaining game against the 1998 champions, France. The match was played on a sunny day in Bloemfontein, and it was the type of football the nation had been hoping for all along. South Africa beat France 2-1. Although it was not good enough to progress to the next round, who could imagine a world in which Bafana Bafana would outshine Les Bleus?

It was incredible. Back in 1998, Doctor Khumalo's Bafana Bafana had lost South Africa's first ever World Cup game 3-0 to host country France. Now, 12 years later, Teko Modise's Bafana Bafana beat France 2-1 in Bloemfontein. The city was set alight that night. The streets did not go to sleep. The sound of vuvuzelas rang through the night air. The nation was proud.

Still, the joy was short-lived. The 3-0 loss to Uruguay had killed Bafana Bafana, and South Africa now held the record for being the only host nation to be knocked out in the group stages of a World Cup. Despite the respectable performance, South Africa is a proud sporting nation and anything short of perfection puts the country into a depression.

'I don't think I had a bad tournament; I didn't have a great one but there were some good moments. The pressure on me was crazy; people blamed everything on me after that tournament. I think I would have played so well if I was just more relaxed. If I could have just played with freedom and had fun, then I know I would have had a different tournament. All I can say is that we were very well prepared for that tournament. We did our best. The World Cup is just a different stage, though. Nothing can prepare you for something that big.'

CHAPTER 18

No wedding cake

Teko met Felicia at a braai in Soweto. A friend thought they would be a good match so they were introduced and shortly afterwards exchanged numbers. It took a while for the numbers to materialise into anything.

They dated during Teko's career with Orlando Pirates. Felicia was not a love-at-first-sight kind of woman in Teko's eyes. They got along well and enjoyed each other's company, but in all honesty Teko felt he was still getting to know her. Things were progressing nice and slowly.

A year after they had started dating, Teko was driving home from training, stuck in traffic and staring out at the Johannesburg sunset when he received a call. *The call.*

Felicia was on the other end of the line. She told Teko that she had fallen pregnant with his child.

Teko had imagined this predicament before and thought through what ought to happen. He had reasoned to himself that, should he make someone pregnant, the right thing to do would be to marry the woman.

When Teko received the phone call his first emotion was anger. He was mad at himself for impregnating a woman he didn't even know that well. He was mad at himself for being irresponsible.

'It wasn't the kind of situation where I planned for Felicia to be the mother of my child and my wife. It kind of just happened, but then it had to be her.'

For Teko, having an abortion was not an option on the table. He said that Felicia and he never discussed it.

'I knew at the time that, irrespective of who the woman was, I was never going to suggest or try to persuade someone else to get an abortion. At the time, I was frightened. I was scared of so many things. I made so many of my decisions out of fear. I didn't think things through. Every time I did something, I was scared of how the public would receive me. I would end up choosing what I thought looked right rather than what I wanted to do. At the time, I knew I wasn't ready to have a child, but I was scared that if I suggested an abortion she would go to the media. At the time I was just trying to portray this image and brand of a South African footballer and not actually leading my life the way I wanted.'

Felicia was well along in her pregnancy when she and Teko married. There was no big ceremony. They didn't have a big party with friends and family and didn't go through the stress of wedding planning. No venue was chosen and no flower girl assigned. No one walked Felicia down the aisle, and no one made a speech for Teko. It was not the happiest day of their lives.

Teko likens this time of his life to someone dropping a plate that shatters into a thousand tiny pieces, and instead of picking them up one by one, he grabs a broom and sweeps them under the carpet.

Everything happened very quickly. Teko was caught between conflicting emotions; he knew that having this baby and marrying Felicia was not something that had been planned, but at the same time he had a burning desire to make a family and to provide them with a more stable life than he had experienced.

Teko told himself, 'The situation is what it is and it ain't what it ain't. I need to accept it and in the midst of accepting it I also need to try to make it work.'

Teko never had a chance to really get to know Felicia as well as a couple about to get married should know each other. He admits that the decisions they made did not come from the heart but arose out of the situation.

Teko always loved the name 'Paballo'. The name means 'hope'

or 'perseverance' and for him it embodied his current relationship.

When Paballo Modise was born Teko was present in the hospital. The doctor asked Teko if he would like to be in the room when she was born. He said no. He gets very uneasy and lightheaded around blood and has an innate fear of doctors and medical rooms. He waited outside and ordered breakfast at the cafeteria. Midway through his eggs he got a phone call from a doctor saying that his daughter had been born. Teko stayed with Paballo and Felicia in the hospital the whole day and through the night.

That day also changed the way Teko thought about his relationship with his new wife. He realised later that when their baby was not around, he found it difficult to be with Felicia. But because he had committed to the marriage for Paballo's sake he needed to make it work.

The house was, however, not built on solid foundations. The truth of the matter was that he and Felicia had married for the wrong reasons. Teko spent much of this time feeling very angry at himself.

Teko's career was also suffering; it felt impossible to make both marriage and career work at the same time. Teko realised that something had to give.

'I was still having difficulties with Orlando Pirates. The papers were after my neck. I was okay with being at war when I left home, I expected it, but when you get home as a married person, you look for peace. When you are not even at peace in your own house, then you need to make changes.'

Teko had worked so hard his whole life to grow his footballing career, he felt unwilling to sacrifice it for a relationship that was not even built on love.

On April fool's day 2010 Teko was chatting to a friend on the phone and something slipped out his mouth for the first time. 'I want to get a divorce.'

He had never actually said the words before but when he did he felt a weight lift off his shoulders.

The friend, conscious of the date, just said, 'You are full of jokes Teko, I'll call you tomorrow.'

That phone call stuck with Teko. Saying he wanted a divorce felt like the truth. Understanding this did not come easily or overnight. He was still scared and conscious that he wanted to make the best decision for his child.

For the period of the World Cup, Teko put his personal issues and the divorce on the backburner. He needed to focus on football, but when the tournament was over, he had to face reality again. Teko had to return home to an unhappy house and an unhappy wife.

With his marriage falling apart, Teko felt as though his biggest problems arose from the smallest issues at home. Under pressure with what seemed like bigger stuff, things big enough to be on the front page of newspapers, he felt like he didn't need to deal with problems at home too.

Eventually, Teko sat Felicia down and told her he thought it was time to separate.

'Having that discussion with Felicia was not difficult at all. At the time she could also see our problems. It was clear that I wasn't the husband I was supposed to be. She was not surprised by me asking for a divorce.'

Teko's main concern was that they manage the proceedings quietly. He asked her what she wanted out of the divorce and said he would grant it to her. She agreed to keep the divorce out of the media. She did not keep this promise.

What followed was the most difficult period of Teko's career. Felicia's friends persuaded her that she could get more out of the divorce if she made it public. The things she would go on to say in the media would force a number of Teko's sponsors to drop him as a player.

'The things she started saying in the media were scary and crazy.'

In the public realm she claimed that Teko no longer financially supported their child, she claimed that he had taken their daughter off medical aid and, to top it all off, she claimed that Teko was an abusive husband.

She later admitted to Teko that she regretted saying the things she said in the media, but by then the damage was already done.

Luckily, Jazzman, as always, was very supportive at this time. He organised counselling for Teko, who was still employed as a professional footballer. Regardless of what was happening at home, if you don't perform as a footballer, you stand the risk of losing some important people a lot of important money. You may soon find yourself out of a job as well as a relationship. Jazzman's fatherly guidance during the time of Teko's divorce is something that changed their relationship forever; Jazzman had become much more than just Teko's agent.

Football itself got tougher for Teko following the divorce. Now, when he was playing, he could hear the supporters voicing their opinions about his failed marriage. They would shout and scream at him. Until now, Teko has never spoken publicly of his divorce. At the time, the only news the fans were getting was by watching Felicia making outrageous claims on TV.

Teko remembers confiding in a friend at the time, 'You know, sometimes we see people who have committed suicide and we call them cowards, but you need to be in that situation to realise that nothing matters any more.' That is not to say that Teko was suicidal; he was not. But he felt that helplessness, the loneliness and the lack of meaning in his life. He understood the mind frame.

It was also difficult to separate his professional and personal lives. The supporters were relentless; they were on his case and ready to impale his head on a spike. He was battling two beasts at once.

'The only thing that could help me, the only thing that gave me protection, was alcohol or staying indoors. You just don't wanna be seen in that state.'

He became paranoid. Even at training, if he saw a group of teammates laughing, he assumed they were laughing at him. Eventually, at rock bottom, Teko came to a realisation – it was either sink or swim.

'You either let this kill your career or you kill it.' Teko had seen many footballers go down this path and not come back … So many footballers don't come back.

CHAPTER 19

The organisation

'Hello, Teko. My name is Melissa. I am here to protect you and guide you.'

It was a strange call to get on a strange day. Teko had just had a fun-filled day in Pretoria. He was at a car-wash event that Dennis Masina had talked him into attending. Dennis always knew about odd events happening around town. The owner of this car wash turned out to be a crime kingpin and would later be arrested. But for now, he was hosting a party at his car wash with the country's most famous footballer in attendance.

Afterwards, Teko was home and trying to switch on the television. He was slightly tipsy so even this was proving difficult.

His phone rang.

Private number.

Teko was bored and drunk so he decided to answer.

'Hello, Teko.' It was a woman's voice. A very familiar voice that Teko had definitely heard before but he couldn't quite remember where from. 'My name is Melissa. I am here to protect and guide you.'

The woman refused to tell Teko who had sent her or what she was meant to be protecting him from.

'You're wasting my time,' Teko said. 'I'm dropping this call now.'

Teko had many people from all walks of life telling him how they could guide him to greatness and how they had the solution to

The organisation

all his problems. As far as he was concerned, this was just another false prophet.

The phone rang again.

'Listen, Teko,' Melissa said quickly, 'what I'm going to tell you will shock you, but I think it's important. Otherwise you will never take me seriously.'

'Okay ... Shoot,' Teko replied, feeling slightly curious and having nothing better to do.

The woman began describing the layout of Teko's house to him over the phone. 'You are sitting on your brown couch right now. Next to you is a window that doesn't have a curtain ...' she carried on describing a number of the items in the house.

Teko knew that he had hosted many people at his house. He was still not buying whatever this lady was selling. 'You've obviously been to my house before for a party or something, that's how you know all these things.'

The woman chuckled and then paused. 'Okay, Teko. I can see I'm not going to get through to you tonight. Sleep well.'

Teko dropped the call, watched some TV and went to sleep.

The next morning, Teko woke up and got ready for training. Before heading over to Orlando Pirates, he had to make a stop at the shopping centre to return some DVDs he had rented. After dropping the movies off and walking out the store, Teko saw a woman arriving to do the same thing. He watched her, mainly because of her car; it was such a beautiful car. The new Range Rover. Teko wanted one just like it. The car was very new in South Africa so Teko took time to stare. He looked at the car and then at the woman; she smiled at Teko and then calmly walked inside.

As Teko got into his car and started towards the training ground, he received a call. It was a private number again, just like the call he had received the previous night.

A woman's voice came through the phone. It was the same woman from the previous night, Melissa. She reminded Teko of their conversation. Teko was barely listening.

'You just saw your dream car, didn't you?' the woman said over the phone.

Teko slowed down a little. Now he was really listening.

'Which dream car?' Teko replied.

'The Range Rover,' she said. 'It was black. There was a woman driving it and she smiled at you.'

Teko began to check over his shoulders.

'So, what now?' Teko asked. 'Are you spying on me or something?'

'No,' Melissa said with a chuckle, 'I'm not spying on you, but I can see everything.'

The conversation ended and the matter remained unresolved and Teko was none the wiser as to who this woman was or why she was calling him.

From that day onwards for the next two years, Teko received a call from this woman named Melissa on a private number. Every. Single. Day. For two years.

Some days, she would call Teko to tell him not to take a particular route when driving to training. Some days she would call to advise him against purchasing something and some days she would call Teko to tell him what was going on in his mind. She would never call when Teko was in the house. However, every time he drove out his gate, he would receive a call from the same private number.

'Listen, I know you're going to Soweto,' she would tell him, even though Teko would not have told anyone that he planned on going to Soweto that day. 'Don't take your usual route there. There is going to be a broken-down car and some roadblocks.' Teko dropped the call and went his usual route. He was met with broken-down cars and roadblocks.

It was a very dark time, emotionally, for Teko. He was vulnerable. It was at the time when his beloved Orlando Pirates had him training by himself. He was drinking more and playing less. It was made even more confusing by the daily calls from a strange woman telling him things that nobody else knew about him. Telling him about stuff he had thought but never verbalised.

She would never tell Teko about his games, if and how he would play or what the result would be. She would only tell Teko about life in general.

The organisation

One day, when Teko was still married and living in Roodepoort, he was dressing up and getting ready to go out. His friend from Kaizer Chiefs, Siboniso Gaxa, was hosting a house party.

Once Teko was ready, he hopped into his new BMW M3 and headed out. The M3 was only two days old. It was the first time Teko had bought a brand-new car. He had taken such delight in watching them peel the plastic off the seats before he drove it off the show-room floor. As he drove out the house he received another phone call. It was Melissa once again.

'Listen to me, Teko, don't go to this party.'

Teko started laughing.

'I'm not joking. Don't go to this party at your friend's house. If you do, your car will give you problems when you wake up in the morning.'

'How is my car going to give me problems?' Teko asked. 'The car is brand new; it won't give me any problems.'

'Just trust me, Teko. Don't go to the party.'

'Okay, cool, I won't go.' Teko dropped the call, switched off his phone and went to the party.

Teko had a nice time at the party. He got to see a number of his friends and when it came time to leave at two o'clock in the morning, Teko headed straight home and climbed into bed. When he woke up in the morning, he started packing his bag and getting ready for training. His wife came into the house looking concerned.

'What's wrong with your car?' she asked.

'Nothing is wrong with my car.'

'Okay, come take a look then.'

Teko was worried; he remembered the phone call he had received the night before. Teko was shocked when he went outside to look at the car. His brand-new M3 had been vandalised beyond recognition. The car was undrivable. Someone had taken a sharp object and scratched the paint off. They had engraved all sorts of insults, swear words and phallic symbols onto the car. There was no way he could drive the car in public.

Felicia wanted answers from Teko as to why his car looked the way it did.

It was at this point that Teko began to take the calls from this private number very seriously.

Later on, as the phone calls continued, Melissa started talking to Teko about joining the 'organisation'. She kept referring to whatever this thing was as an organisation. One day, she emailed Teko forms to fill out.

Due to the desperate nature of Teko's situation and his need to do anything to improve his life, he was seriously considering joining whatever this organisation was. He printed the forms at home and filled them out, but noticed something odd. The forms had no name, emblem or logo – just directions to a church where they were to be handed in.

Teko convinced a friend to come with him, so one day they got in his car and followed the directions to a church situated far away in between nothing and nowhere. When they arrived at the church, Teko was taken aback. There were a number of people there, all of them white people dressed in black.

It seemed as though they had been expecting Teko. He stood there, motionless, with his forms in his hand. The congregation informed Teko that the office was closed for the day so they could not take his forms.

In the days that followed, Teko received many calls from the organisation explaining their ethos and what they stood for. This happened to coincide with a time when many stories were circulating on social media about secret societies. The newspaper conspiracy theorists were going crazy about a so-called connection between hip-hop icons Beyoncé and Jay-Z and the Illuminati.

'So, you guys are the Illuminati, hey?' Teko asked Melissa when she called one day.

'No, we are an organisation.'

'Why me? What do you guys need from me that you want me to join?'

'We need a footballer, Teko. We've never had a soccer player before.'

'What's in it for me?'

'Wealth, Teko. We guarantee you a lifetime of wealth.'

The organisation

They never explained to Teko what was required of him and she was vague on many details.

'How will you guarantee me wealth?'

'We can't tell you that until you join, Teko. You need to fill out the forms, get registered, and then some men will come to your house to interview your wife. After that you just need to attend meetings.'

A friend spoke to Teko one day when he was on the verge of joining.

'Teko, how badly do you need this money they are offering you, my friend?'

'Not badly, but everyone could use a little extra cash.'

Teko confesses that this particular friend hasn't had a lot of experience in life but, that day, his wisdom shone true and bright.

'Look, Teko, I don't know how this whole thing works, but the chances are that these guys are going to need you to sacrifice something. Nothing comes free in this world. I don't know if this is a church but every church requires some kind of sacrifice. There is something they are not telling you. They are not telling you what you have to sacrifice because they want you to join. Once you have joined and you are in …' His friend took a long pause. 'Who knows, Teko? Who knows what will happen to you? You will have to follow their rules and you are not a rules guy. Look at you; you can't even follow Orlando Pirates' rules. You are meant to be at training but you are here with me now. You don't know what's on the other side of this door, Teko.'

That advice stuck with Teko like a guiding light. He started hesitating about handing in the forms. Sensing his hesitation, the organisation stepped up their efforts to get Teko to join. He was relaxing at a friend's house in the middle of the day when he got another call from the private number.

'You need to drive out of that place you are in. Drive to the nearest bank, a Nedbank, and draw all the money out of your account.'

'Listen,' Teko said with a chuckle, 'that bank account I have with Nedbank is empty. I haven't used it in years.'

'Teko. Listen. Go. Now.'

Teko drove out and located the nearest Nedbank. It was 15 minutes before the bank closed. Teko was still hesitant to go in and draw all the money out of his account, so he decided to go to the ATM, draw a small amount of money and check the balance to see what he was dealing with.

The bank closed its doors while Teko was making the withdrawal. He withdrew R1000 and looked at his receipt. There was R99 000 left in the account that was previously empty. They had deposited R100 000 for him.

As he looked down at his receipt with his mouth wide open in shock, his phone rang again.

'You didn't listen to me. I told you to take all the money out of that account. That money will be gone tomorrow because you didn't listen.'

That moment truly stung Teko Modise; the fact that through all this mystery and all this talk of 'wealth', all he ever got out of it was R1000.

Teko, driving to McDonald's one day in the midst of his divorce, answered the private number for the last time.

'Listen. This is the last time I'm going to speak to you guys so I'm going to be nice to you. Don't ever call or contact me again. I'm going through a divorce and I want nothing to do with you guys. Since you came into my life, nothing good has happened. I need to stand up and beat my demons by myself.'

'You sure this is what you want?'

'Yeah.'

Teko hung up the phone and later changed his number. He was keen to resume a normal life, but normal was going to be more difficult to achieve than he would have liked.

It would not be the last time a weird force like this would enter his life.

CHAPTER 20

The king from Congo

Teko was discovering an unfortunate pattern in his life. Only at his lowest point did people try to get something from him. When he was in his darkest hour, that's when the vultures swooped in.

The papers were filled with stories about the 'Curse of Teko'. It used to be the case that Teko was always the best player at a club that was struggling to win trophies; now he was not even the best player. The whole country frowned in his direction and the media painted him as yet another failed star lost to ill-discipline and bad luck.

'I'm not from a place where there are kings. I'm from the hood.'

This was Teko's reaction when he heard that there was a king from Congo who wished to meet with him. This king had apparently been hellbent on finding Teko. He was a very powerful and wealthy king and offered money to anyone who could find and bring him the one-and-only Teko Modise.

Teko was curious about this king, so he went to his house, as invited. The king's house was in the posh Johannesburg suburb of Houghton. It seemed to be one of those houses brimming with activity and visitors all day every day.

He was curious as to why he was there and what the king wanted with him. The king, in return, seemed ecstatic to have the legendary Teko Modise in his house. Teko had absolutely no idea how big of a deal this king was.

'He just said he was a king, but it's easy for anybody to say that they are a king,' Teko recalls with a shrug of his shoulders.

The house was magnificent and the king was obviously wealthy. Teko was not the only one visiting that day. The house was full of foreigners, and Teko noticed something strange immediately – there were no women in the house. It was strictly a men-only affair.

It soon became clear that this was no normal king. Whenever one of the many male visitors would address the king, they would bow before him as a sign of respect. When they wanted to approach the king, instead of walking to him, they would crawl.

The king, not wanting to overwhelm Teko with too much strangeness on the first day, tried to hide all of this. He waved people away from bowing and scraping, but they would not. It was part of their culture to bow to the king.

The king didn't want Teko to feel intimidated; he just wanted him to relax and play some pool. He delighted in getting his guests to play against each other and then against him, even giving money away as his guests played. If someone sank a really difficult shot, the king would give him some cash. If someone pocketed a trick shot, the king would give him cash. If someone missed a trick shot, he would give cash for trying anyway.

Teko never found out why he was there that first day, but he enjoyed himself and walked away with a little cash. One of his friends came and fetched him when he was ready to leave.

'Mfwethu, you are very lucky,' Teko's friend said to him.

'And why is that now?'

'People are giving you money just for relaxing and playing pool.'

Teko had seen this movie before, 'It won't be that simple. There is a catch to this whole thing. Watch, my friend.'

The king called Teko the following day and told him that he would be free around seven o'clock that evening. He told Teko he should visit once again.

Teko began asking around about the king. He knew a few Congolese nationals and upon mentioning the king's name, they shuddered with excitement. He was supposedly no ordinary king. His power was unparalleled and those who Teko spoke to said he was lucky to be in the presence of this king as he had very strong spiritual connections. This king was famous in Congo for the strength and effectiveness of his muti. He had contact with the ancestors and the power of his ability to summon good or bad fortune was unmatched.

The king began telling Teko about his work, how his spirituality was his guiding force. He spoke about TP Mazembe, a Congolese football team famous for muti and off-the-pitch methods of winning games.

Teko noticed that very important people would come visit the king from Congo. There were always fancy cars outside, and whoever would visit would bring the king a bottle of the finest alcohol you could pull off the shelves. Johnnie Walker Blue Label, Veuve Clicquot ... the best of the bottles.

Teko still did not know what this all-powerful king wanted with him, but he said something that made the hairs on Teko's neck stand to attention.

'You know, Teko. Me, I don't sacrifice human beings. That's the difference between some people and me. They sacrifice in blood, but that's not me.'

Thoughts of the previous two years with Melissa's regular phone calls came rushing back. Teko was scared once again. He began asking questions: Why am I here at this guy's house? What does this all have to do with me? I'm just a footballer. Maybe this guy just wants my T-shirt? I will sign my T-shirt and leave it here, whatever this guy wants.

The king still would not tell Teko exactly what it was that he wanted with him. He did mention the 'Curse of Teko' a lot though, and he made it out like he could help. Again, this was far from the first time Teko had heard such a statement. The king said he could not give Teko all his attention that day, as he still had business to attend to ...

'We'll speak tomorrow when I have less to do.' The king left it at that.

The Curse of Teko Modise

The next day Teko returned to the king's house. The king asked Teko about the new Range Rover Millar. He wanted Teko to tell him how much the car cost. Teko had no idea. They googled it and found out that the Range Rover cost roughly R2 million. This made the king want it even more. He had a fascination with cars. The king really liked the Jeep that Teko was driving and told Teko that he had tried to go out and buy the same model that same day. The king was shocked when the car dealer turned down his offer because the king wanted to pay for the car in cash, upfront.

'Why do they not take cash for cars in South Africa?' the king asked Teko, genuinely disturbed. 'In Congo, you put the cash on the table and drive the car out the store. In South Africa, they want the bank involved and all this nonsense.'

The king talked more about money and the material things in life. Teko listened for most of it without saying much.

The conversation limped on and on until the king eventually focused on the 'Curse of Teko'. He dwelt on the spiritual aspect and made it clear that there was no curse that could not be undone, especially when using his almighty power.

The king proceeded to tell Teko about the curse and how it was preventing him from reaching his true potential as a footballer. The king said he could help Teko; he said that in a recent dream the spirits came to tell him to help.

'I was listening,' Teko admits, 'but I've heard this story before. Everyone thinks they can help me. I even told him so. I had hoped that he would be different to everyone else but that didn't seem to be the case.'

The king protested. 'This is different, Teko. All I need is time and privacy. I need you to trust me.'

The king led Teko into some kind of medicine room.

'I think he did all his work from this room. It was a dark room, a very dark room … A very, very dark room. It was filled with ornaments, wooden statues; it even had things that were dead. It was the most scared I have ever been. That was a room that … No one would ever go in there.'

Teko took a seat in the room. The king moved around and

started chanting and singing. He was performing the rituals in a language that Teko did not understand. He darted from corner to corner, singing and chanting.

The king eventually turned around and addressed Teko. He told him to close his eyes.

'In the back of my mind, I was thinking, okay, I will close my eyes knowing that I may very well open them again. I don't want to see something I can't forget.'

Teko did as he was told and closed his eyes. The chanting from the king intensified. As the chanting got louder, Teko realised that there was not only one voice in the room. Sounds began coming from all corners, not just any noises, shouting and screaming in a foreign language. Teko realised the other voices were coming from the ornaments and wooden sculptures. They had begun chanting. The lifeless objects had come to life under the command of the king's rituals.

Teko did not recognise the language that the ornaments were speaking to the king. He knew it was not French, though. To say Teko was frightened out of his socks at this point would be an understatement. He remained dead still and waited for this terrifying moment to end.

The voices gradually died down. The conversation between the objects and the king had been long and Teko was prepared for anything that might come next.

Teko opened his eyes and the king began addressing him again. He started outlining the rituals Teko should do to rid himself of the curse. He had very particular instructions for Teko. The king ordered him to buy a red cloth and a white cloth and sit on them in a certain manner. Many muti instructions were similar to this so Teko was not too disturbed by the order. What came next, however, was something Teko found more unusual.

'I have to give you a gift,' the king said bluntly to Teko.

He went to a corner of the room and retrieved a box. It was the same size and shape of a shoebox but it was metal and worn in appearance. The king slid open the metal box and showed Teko the interior. Nothing. It was empty. He closed the box again and

The Curse of Teko Modise

ordered Teko to place his hand on top. The king then put his hand on top of Teko's and began chanting once more. He blew on top of the box and then placed it down gently.

The king opened the box again and inside was a real, breathing, living rabbit. A white rabbit. The rabbit was so white that its colour shocked Teko a little more than the fact that it had appeared in an empty metal box.

The king reached in and gently picked up the whiter-than-white rabbit and placed it on the floor next to Teko.

'That rabbit just chilled there,' Teko recalls in disbelief. 'Most rabbits will run away from humans. That one just sat completely still next to me.'

After a long pause, the king looked from the rabbit to Teko and gave him further instructions.

'Take this rabbit. It is a gift. Make sure you look after it. Make sure it is fed. It eats carrots, but you can't feed it any carrots you get from the store. You must come here to buy the carrots for your rabbit.'

'I was worried,' Teko recalls. 'A rabbit is a commitment and I know I have commitment issues. The week I had to take care of that rabbit was the longest week of my life. That rabbit eats a lot! And I still had to pay for the damn "special" carrots.'

A couple of days later, the king informed Teko that his help was no longer for free. He guaranteed that he could rid Teko of the curse but, like any other customer, Teko had to pay. He offered Teko a discounted rate of R50 000. The king specified that Teko was to withdraw the R50 000 from a bank, change the cash into US dollars, put the dollars in an envelope and deliver it to his mansion in Houghton.

Teko made his way to the bank.

'When you are in a dark place you will do anything to get out,' Teko admits in hindsight.

At the bank, Teko's friend was passionately against what was going on. He begged Teko to see reason.

'Chief! You can't do this. These people almost tricked you once before and now you are going to let them do it to you again.'

'Mfwethu, these are dark times,' Teko told his friend. 'It's survival of the fittest now. Let's just do this thing. It's only R50 000. We will make it back someday somehow.'

Teko withdrew the money, changed it into dollars at the teller and placed the thick wad of cash in a brown envelope. They drove carefully to the Houghton mansion. The king had informed Teko that he was out of town on business on that particular day but his assistant would be able to help.

When they arrived, the first problem became evident: the assistant could barely speak a word of English or any other language that Teko spoke. Nonetheless, after football, money is probably the most universal language so the assistant grabbed the envelope in Teko's hand and opened it.

Teko and his friend stood back and crossed their arms while they watched the assistant pull the cash out of the envelope. He carefully studied every note and counted the whole wad. He put the notes back, pulled them out again and counted them again. He was being very careful and making sure it was all there. Once he was satisfied he had counted just right, he took the notes and placed them in a pot on the desk beside him. Next, he took a bottle of gasoline and began to pour some of it over the notes in the pot. Teko barely had enough time to react before the assistant had lit a match and thrown it in the pot with the money.

Teko and his friend jumped backwards and screamed in horror. Their faces lit up with shock as they watched R50 000 burning to ashes. Teko could not lift his jaw off the floor long enough to say anything. It wouldn't have helped anyway; the money was burnt and the assistant still could not speak English.

The assistant proceeded to sweep up all the ashes and place them in a metal box. Teko recognised it as the same metal box that his rabbit had come out of. When the assistant closed the box, the loss of Teko's R50 000 became a reality. The ashes had disappeared when the assistant opened the box again.

That was the final straw for Teko. He realised that enough was enough. He realised he was slipping back into the same hole that he had worked so hard to climb out of for the past two years. He realised that none of these people could help him. Only he could help himself.

'I realised I could not do this to myself any more. I needed to concentrate on the single thing I love the most: football. If I win then I win and if I lose then I lose. Either way, I needed to come back down to reality.'

Teko tried to distance himself from the king. He blocked him from his social media and changed his number once again. Teko even had to block the king on Snapchat. He found himself asking, 'What kind of king has Snapchat anyway?'

Teko has no doubt that the appearance of the king and the phone calls from Melissa are in some way connected. To this day, Teko has no idea what any of these people wanted from him or why they contacted him.

'All I know is that if it has happened twice before, then I am sure that it will happen again. The question I keep asking myself is, why me? Sometimes it really troubles me that I don't know the answer to that question.'

CHAPTER 21

The ridiculous suit

Back in a more familiar world Teko still managed to rub his team and coach up the wrong way, and one of the biggest irritations concerned his car. And not just any car, his pride and joy, a James Bond car, the Aston Martin DB9. Teko added to the problems of his relationship with the club by driving the car to an Orlando Pirates training session. The relationship between Teko and the club was really difficult at this stage, and the sight and sound of a DB9 rolling into the parking lot with Teko inside was guaranteed to ruffle feathers.

It wasn't long before he was called into the head office.

'You can't drive that car to training,' the officials told him. 'The other players will see that and think that we are paying you too much; it won't be long before they all come around demanding higher salaries.'

He had been training behind the goalposts for about a year and a half now. That meant he was running less than all of the other players, he was less fit and less motivated. After all this, he thought to himself: I'm on the sidelines watching my career pass me by, so whatever, I'm going to do whatever I want to.

In defiance of instructions, he started driving the Aston Martin to training again. Teko hadn't played a game for Pirates in a very long time and was in a vicious routine. He would drive to training in the morning, run around behind the goalposts, buy booze on

The Curse of Teko Modise

the way home and sit and drink in his garage.

Every day this happened.

Go to training, go home and drink.

Wake up, go to training, go home and drink.

Wake up, go to training, go home and drink.

One Wednesday Coach Ruud Krol approached Teko at training.

'I want you to train with the team tomorrow,' Ruud said. 'Come out from behind the goalposts.'

Teko saw what was happening, and thought that he was being set up. Even though Teko's relationship with Pirates management might have been deteriorating, the supporters still loved him. He was their superstar and they were beginning to ask why he wasn't being played.

Ruud needed to justify why he was excluding Teko. He also knew what bad habits Teko had developed in the last couple of months but he decided to play him anyway.

Teko spotted the danger in the situation, so that day after training he drove straight past the bottle store and proceeded to the gym where he trained for an extra two hours. He was very unfit.

The next day, there was still no indication of whether Teko would be playing on the weekend. But by the weekend, Teko's name was on the list for the starting XI. Orlando Pirates were due to take on Moroka Swallows in Dobsonville at three o'clock on Sunday. It was December. Anyone who has been to Dobsonville at three o'clock in December will know the excruciating, intense and unforgiving heat that bakes off the dry Soweto field.

'Now imagine,' Teko recalls, 'I had been drinking for four months and these guys put me in a game at three o'clock in Dobsonville.'

It was a high-pressure game. Moroka Swallows vs Orlando Pirates is the original Soweto derby; this game had been played for many years before the birth of Kaizer Chiefs; the whole country was watching.

Dobsonville Stadium did not have an empty chair in sight.

Ruud Krol left Teko on the field for the entire 90 minutes of

The ridiculous suit

the game. It was a gruelling affair with non-stop running. Orlando Pirates emerged with 2-1 as victors. Teko Modise was named Man of the Match.

Teko was simply sensational that day. Through all the pain, lack of fitness and unrelenting heat, he pushed through and gave one of the best performances of his career.

After the Moroka Swallows game, Jazzman told Teko something very important: 'Listen, Teko, just realise one thing: there are only two other clubs in this country that can afford you – Kaizer Chiefs or Mamelodi Sundowns. Just make sure, wherever you go, that you are ready. Wherever you go, you will need to justify your price tag and you will have to be ready to play immediately. People will want to prove that you are overrated; you need to prove them wrong.'

Believing that he would be leaving Pirates soon, Teko was feeling good about things. He was not a particularly popular guy at the Pirates training at the time, but he didn't particularly care either. He said to the other Pirates players, 'Guys, I'm going to play against you someday soon. I will be leaving this club. I know you guys are going to play dirty against me. I know you guys are going to try kicking me. I know the coaches will tell you to kick me, but that's fine. I don't mind. Enjoy your last training sessions with me. I'll be gone soon.'

The other Pirates players laughed at Teko. They knew he was going to either Chiefs or Sundowns. They told him that he would be furniture at those clubs, meaning he would see less game time than he did at Pirates; they told him that he would sit on the bench and gather dust, nothing more than a brand ambassador for the club.

It meant little to Teko, though – he knew he was on his way out. Jazzman called him one evening, informing him that Sundowns wanted his services.

On the phone that evening, Jazzman was very direct with Teko: 'Hey, Teko, do you have a suit?'

'Jazz, I've got plenty of suits,' Teko replied.

'Okay, good. Tomorrow, we have a meeting at nine in the

morning. I don't know exactly what is going to happen. Irvin Khoza is going to be there and the press are going to be there too. They may release you from the club or they may not. All I know is that you need to look the part – wear a suit.'

Teko had a good, long think about what he was going to wear. The more he thought about it the more he realised that he did nothing by the book. He was no ordinary guy. He thought that, seeing as his stay had been nothing short of controversial, he was going to go out with a bang.

He chose the most obnoxious, outrageous, brightly coloured suit he could find. It was more than offensive to the eyes. He wore a pink shirt, a red tie, and all the other colours he could throw together. It ticked all the wrong boxes.

'I loved it. I did it on purpose; I wanted to go out in style.'

The next day Teko arrived for the meeting. He imagined the meeting taking place in a big room with all of South Africa watching and Jazzman, his protector, by his side.

When he arrived, there were a couple of people gathered outside the meeting room. There were members of the media, Orlando Pirates officials, and Jazzman. The door of the room opened; Irvin Khoza glanced at Teko and summoned him inside.

Teko was hoping Jazzman would be invited in too. He was not. It was just the Iron Duke, Teko Modise, and his ridiculous suit, which was starting to look like a bad decision now that he was face to face with the most powerful man in South African football.

'If there is one thing you can pray for in this life, it's that you never find yourself alone in a room with the Iron Duke when he is angry.'

And Irvin truly was furious. He told Teko that he was disrespectful and that all of his actions over the past while were wrong. The grilling went on for an hour while the media waited outside.

Teko was wondering how they expected him to act after all he had been through. 'The worst part about it, though,' Teko recalls, 'is that I don't have a father. I didn't even have a father figure or an advisor. The only person I could turn to for help was Jazzman and

The ridiculous suit

sometimes it's not enough hearing advice from the same person.'

His behaviour may have been rash, but he didn't know any better. He had no one to advise him and he had difficulty learning from his mistakes.

Irvin told Teko that he would release him on one condition: he was not allowed to join Kaizer Chiefs. After that, Irvin pushed his chair back and stood up. The ground shook as he made his way past Teko to the door, opened it and summoned the media and Jazzman inside with a much more welcoming tone than he had given Teko for the past hour.

Once everyone was seated and settled down, Irvin began to speak: 'We have decided to stop all investigations into the misdemeanours and behaviour of Teko Modise and we will be releasing him from his contract with Orlando Pirates with immediate effect.'

CHAPTER 22

A rocky start

'It was probably the toughest decision of my footballing career. Everything was coming undone. I was losing two things at once. I was losing my wife and I was losing Orlando Pirates. A team that I love, a team that I have given everything for, and I've got the scars to prove it. It was difficult to walk away from them. It was a difficult time. However, this is where I was tested. This was when I showed my worth; this is when I showed my resilience.'

Teko had to pull himself out of rock bottom.

'I remember after the World Cup, I felt that I didn't play according to expectations. I don't think I played bad but it was not good enough for my standards. The first thing I did after coming out of the World Cup camp was to go and buy a car, my dream car, the Aston Martin. Being in that car helped me to forget a lot of things; everyone's focus shifted from my bad World Cup to my new car.'

The car was the source of a lot of controversy and the papers were running wild with stories about Teko's lavish lifestyle. Jazzman, too, heard of these stories and gave Teko a call one day: 'Hey, man, did you buy an Aston Martin?'

'No, I didn't, Jazzman.'

'Okay, sharp, I'm coming over to your house now.'

Teko had to quickly drive his new Aston Martin out of the garage, park it down the road somewhere and walk back to his house. By the time Jazzman arrived at Teko's place, there was no Aston Martin in the driveway. Jazzman has never seen that car to this day, except on social media.

The car caused so many issues for Teko. Jazzman hated it (even though Teko denied having it), Orlando Pirates hated it and it was becoming more of a burden than a blessing. Teko made the smart choice and sold his dream car.

Over the December holidays, Teko confided in his friend and former Pirates teammate Dennis Masina, 'I'm probably moving to Sundowns in January. I'm telling you that I am going to become a different player. I won't do the things I was doing at Pirates.'

Teko was in the position where he needed to prove a point. The public at large had written Teko off as another failed superstar, full of potential but ill-disciplined.

'I enjoy pressure. I enjoyed the fact that all eyes were on me. I liked that everyone wanted to see me as a failure. I loved that I had the opportunity to prove them wrong. I thrive on it. I decided that when I get to my new club, I would become a different kind of player.'

The football world is cruel. If Teko did not pick himself up and dust himself off right there and then after that final press conference with Irvin Khoza then he would forever be remembered (or forgotten) as the Orlando Pirates legend-turned-villain.

The press conference was short and to the point. Irvin ran the show ... Teko had nothing to add; he did not give a media statement. The journalists were, naturally, filled to the brim with questions. They wanted to know where Teko was going next. He kept a straight face and a closed mouth, not because he wanted to keep it a secret, but because, at the time, he himself did not even know his next destination. Of course, he could not let the reporters know that – he had to appear in control.

The media began writing about the 'Curse of Teko' again. That's mainly why they wanted to know his next destination. They were not worried about what it would do for his career; they were concerned about which team would be cursed next.

Orlando Pirates had recently won the 2010 and 2011 MTN8

competitions, and they did so without Teko in the squad. 'You see?' the journalists whispered to each other. 'It is happening again. As soon as he is not around the trophies come back. Who's he going to play for next? Who will fall under the "Curse of Teko"?'

Teko drove home after the press conference. He was tired; he just wanted to get out of his outrageously coloured suit. He was halfway through taking off his bright red tie when Jazzman phoned: 'Pack your things, Teko, let's go to Chloorkop.'

In the Second World War, an airport right next to Chloorkop was famous for being a training base for air-force pilots from around the world. But this wasn't the Second World War, and Teko was no fighter pilot. These days, Chloorkop is known for one thing and one thing only – being the home of Mamelodi Sundowns.

And so, on the very same day as the press conference when Pirates released Teko, Jazzman and Teko set off towards Chloorkop and signed for Sundowns. Once again, Teko was sworn to secrecy.

Teko would have loved to sign for his favourite team from his childhood, Kaizer Chiefs. However, he was under strict instructions from Irvin not to. Kaizer Motaung, the owner of Kaizer Chiefs, and Irvin Khoza were good friends and they didn't like messing with each other's property. More importantly, whether you are on good speaking terms with the Iron Duke or not, one thing remains constant – you never go against his instructions.

So Teko signed for Mamelodi Sundowns. It was a very big deal. Moving from Pirates to Sundowns is the equivalent of moving from Manchester United to Chelsea – they were not mortal enemies, but they were two of the three biggest teams in the league.

Like many other developments in Teko's life, his move to Sundowns was full of action. After he had signed for Sundowns in 2011 and reported for his first training session, keen to impress his new colleagues, he noticed something odd when he tried to leave. The supporters of Mamelodi Sundowns had descended on Chloorkop to make their demands clear to management. The supporters circled the training ground and blocked the entrances and exits. They felt that the team was not operating professionally and they did not like what they had been watching on the

A rocky start

field of play. They demanded that the CEO and coach be fired immediately. Furthermore, they refused to allow any of the players to leave practice as they felt they should be punished for their poor performances.

Luckily for Teko, the supporters reasoned that he was a new player and could not be held responsible for previous performances. He was their new hope, and for now he was free to leave. Teko obliged.

From the beginning of the Sundowns move, Teko's heart was still dreaming of a move overseas. He was still having difficulty reading the world around him and for a while he even thought that Jazzman was somehow in on the 'conspiracy' to prevent his overseas move because he knew how much Jazzman was known to like Orlando Pirates.

Jazzman thought that it was wisest not to entertain any such unsettled thinking and, once again, he took a back seat and waited for the dust to settle. A while later he and Teko spent a day of reconciliation together, working on building their relationship. To build trust, Jazzman came up with a new rule for his organisation, and from that day forward any deal he does is done with the player in the room at all times, from start to finish. His players from that day on would be privy to any discussions in the boardroom between agent and chairman.

At some point during that first season, a journalist approached Teko and offered to secure a sponsorship deal for him with Adidas. Without informing Jazzman and while still contracted to Nike, Teko ran out onto the field for Sundowns wearing Adidas boots. It wasn't long before the Nike executives were on the phone to Jazzman asking him how Teko could do such a senseless thing. This made life difficult for Jazzman as he was in the middle of another period where Teko was not answering his phone calls.

Jazzman was fed up. He got in his car, drove over to Chloorkop and waited for Teko to finish training before confronting him. In response, Teko gave Jazzman a long story of what had been promised to him by other people. It broke Jazzman's heart. He realised properly for the first time the number of people who were out to deceive Teko, and how difficult Teko found it to see through the deceivers. Jazzman was shocked at how Teko had handled the Nike situation. The brand had sponsored Teko since before he had become famous and he jumped ship to their rival without even terminating his contract with them.

After that, Jazzman started withdrawing from Teko's life. It was impossible to compete with these vultures; he could not fight the waves of attack any longer. Jazzman had made up his mind: 'Good luck and goodbye, Teko. Whoever you think will help you, I wish you all the best.'

From that point, Jazzman stopped calling. The tables had turned. Now Teko was the one who was chasing Jazzman. It was a wake-up call.

What made Teko's arrival at Mamelodi Sundowns interesting was the faith that was placed on him to elevate the team. The pressure was immense. Soon after his arrival, Teko was handed the captain's armband and the number-10 jersey – a big deal.

It was no ordinary day. They were playing at home against none other than Jomo Cosmos. The Black Prince himself presented Teko with the number-10 jersey. After Jomo, it is widely held that there would never be a number 10 worthy of Jomo's endorsement. In front of the crowd and before his own team, Jomo signed the number-10 jersey and handed it to Teko. It is the only jersey that hangs framed in Teko's house today, and it is the only time Jomo has given such an endorsement of the number 10, the number that he made famous in South Africa.

Teko used to joke with all the legends at the clubs he played at, telling all the men who played in Jomo's era that there were no pictures of them playing, only pictures of them trying to tackle Jomo. SABC used to show old footage of legendary soccer matches, and Teko could see just how great Jomo Sono was. Jomo is, and always will be, the benchmark for greatness.

What eased the pressure for Teko in that first season, however, was the favourable position that Mamelodi Sundowns were in. They are nicknamed the Brazilians, partly because they wear the same colours as the Samba Boys, but also because they can be

A rocky start

downright ruthless on the football pitch. Sundowns have always been one of the top teams in the league. Popularity wise, Kaizer Chiefs and Orlando Pirates are as good as it gets in South Africa, but, statistically, in terms of trophies, games won and goals scored, Mamelodi Sundowns were the kings of South African football.

In Teko's first season at Sundowns, it seemed a given that they would win the league; they had every reason to do so. But anyone who has hung around a football field for any length of time will know that there is no such thing as a sure thing.

Sundowns had four games remaining in the season. They needed six points to secure the league title, so all they needed to do was win two games, or at the very least draw three and win one.

A Zimbabwean named Ian Gorowa was coaching Sundowns at the time. He had been a talented footballer in his day, but later would be handed a 10-year ban by the football association in Zimbabwe for his role in a match-fixing scandal in his home country. However, at this point in our story, Gorowa was just a coach – a very good coach – but something odd started happening towards the end of the season when the trophy looked to be in the bag.

With four games to go in the season, all against smaller teams, Gorowa started changing things unnecessarily. He was placing players out of position, putting strikers on the wing and defenders in the midfield. Some even joked that he would have put Teko as a goalkeeper and himself in the number-10 position if he had it all his way.

Gorowa seemed hellbent on proving a point rather than winning the league. It sometimes seems as if the most important thing for a coach is to constantly prove that he is the big man at the head of the table. This was an especially difficult task at Mamelodi Sundowns where all the players were extremely well-paid celebrities in South Africa.

Gorowa began benching many players, as if to show them who was boss, and Teko was not immune to his behaviour. Gorowa was particularly wary of Teko. When Teko arrived at the club, many had already formed an opinion about him, opinions based

The Curse of Teko Modise

on a set of assumptions that were built on rumours.

Most coaches assume that Teko is going to be trouble, that his head is too big and his jeans sag too low. They all have a theory of how to deal with his 'attitude', which usually involves a lot of discipline and unnecessary punishment.

In his mission to prove a point, Gorowa even went as far as playing certain players he knew had gone out drinking the night before, just so he could watch them suffer in the heat the next day and so that he could show them ... Show them who was boss.

Gorowa had his theories on how to deal with Teko. For example, he would not play Teko in a cup game against Orlando Pirates because he thought there would be too much trouble due to the history between them.

'Having a big name in Africa is a blessing and a curse. When you are younger, everyone wants the best for you. They encourage you and praise you; they want good things to come your way. They love it when you have to beg, but when you get those things, then they want the worst for you. They want to see you fail and be at the bottom again.'

Mamelodi Sundowns' last four games were against Mpumalanga Black Aces, Free State Stars, Amazulu and Maritzburg United – very beatable teams by any standard. They won the first game but lost the last three, meaning that they lost out on the league title by one win. Ruud Krol and Orlando Pirates went on to win the league that season. Not only that, but they won the treble. This is when any team wins three or more trophies in a season. No South African club had ever done it, but Pirates managed to achieve it, once Teko was released. For those who believed in the curse, it couldn't have been scripted better.

Now, you can imagine what the newspapers were saying. The 'Curse of Teko' was no longer just a catch-phrase; it was a headline. Teko was somehow responsible for Mamelodi Sundowns wasting their last six points and losing out on the title. He was also, somehow, responsible for Pirates winning the treble, just by leaving and taking his curse with him.

Pirates kept climbing the ladder from there. Ruud Krol would go on to win the title again the next season. Teko was still trophy-less.

Carlos Alberto Parreira had been replaced by Teko's old coach Pitso Mosimane as the man in charge of the national team. During national duty, Pitso would speak to Teko often about Sundowns; he would ask why they were playing this player or that player or why they weren't playing this or that formation. His interest in Sundowns was unusually intense.

In those days, however, everyone was talking about Sundowns. The once-mighty team was in trouble. The players were not the best of friends with each other and argued often. Even at that early stage, Teko believed that Pitso was probably the only man in the country who could fix the situation, despite what he felt about him personally.

Even though Sundowns was on Pitso's radar, he was not on theirs – not yet, anyway. For now, Sundowns brought in Johan Neeskens to change their fortunes, but regrettably things did not go according to plan.

CHAPTER 23

'Downgrade everything'

After the divorce Teko found himself alone in a big house. He had three cars – very beautiful cars – but they had little practical value and were costing him a fortune to keep. He knew they were unnecessary.

The most difficult thing in the aftermath of Teko's divorce was trust. He simply did not know where it could be found. Teko really wanted to have a family life more stable than the one in which he had grown up. He wanted a family to come home to and a wife to love and be loved by.

One day after training with Mamelodi Sundowns, Teko approached the team doctor, who was also a trusted friend.

'My man,' Teko said to him, 'I am struggling to find a real relationship. I am struggling to find the kind of woman who can see beyond the Teko Modise name. I want something real, genuine friendships and relationships.'

The team doctor thought long and hard about Teko's problems and came up with a solution.

'Look, boss, this thing of you wanting people to see past the Teko Modise name, that's never going to happen. People know you. You are a superstar; that's just the way it is. But there is one thing you can do to test if the people in your life are genuine or not …'

'What's that?' Teko asked.

'Downgrade everything you have.'

Teko took a step backwards out of shock. 'Downgrade? Comrade! You must be confused! For a doctor, it might be fine to downgrade, but I'm a public figure.'

'No, man, I'm being serious, Teko. Downgrade everything. Sell all your cars and buy a smaller car. Sell your mansion and buy a smaller house. Downgrade everything in your life and then see what kind of relationships and friendships you attract.'

The doctor was making sense, so Teko listened, and decided to act on the advice.

While it was difficult to sell his house, he managed to sell his cars. At the time, he had a BMW M3, a BMW 1 Series and a Jeep SRT8. He sold the two BMWs but held onto the Jeep. He loved that Jeep. He used to use it for family matters; now he also drove it to training.

Selling the two BMWs was no clean break, though. Teko still owed the bank some money for those vehicles and had to pay the difference before he was finally clear of the cars.

When Teko arrived at practice one day, the doctor who had advised him was walking past the car park. He saw Teko's Jeep. The doctor dropped his bag, and it hit the floor at the same time as his jaw. He waited for Teko to step out the car before confronting him.

'Hey, wena! You didn't listen. I told you to sell all your cars, look at this massive car you still have!'

Teko threw his hands up in the air out of protest.

'No, man! I can't sell this one too. What will happen when I'm chilling with my friends? What will they think?'

The doctor shook his head, 'Listen here, Teko, you're not doing this for your friends; you're doing it for yourself and you're doing it for your future.'

Teko sold the Jeep and bought a Golf 6. It was still a beautiful, shiny car, just a little less pricey.

The media, always interested in Teko, discovered what was going on. They saw him driving a Jeep one day and then a Golf the next, so they did what the media does best in the absence of facts – they speculated. Stories started circulating that Teko was obviously in financial trouble. They said that his Jeep and two other cars had been repossessed by the bank. The headlines went crazy: 'TEKO MODISE IS BROKE'.

This is obviously a distressing thing to read about yourself, particularly when you are not in a position to defend yourself.

Teko went back to his team doctor the next day, fuming.

'You see what you've done now!' Teko shouted at him. 'Now everyone is saying that I'm broke. It's embarrassing. They are saying that all my things have been repossessed.'

The doctor remained cool and calm. 'It's fine, Teko. I'll tell you something: your soul hasn't been repossessed. Your conscience is clear; they can't repossess that. They can't take that away from you. You are doing the right thing.'

So Teko continued along his path. He found a small flat. It was lonely but it was serving a purpose. It was just Teko, his Golf 6, and his flat. Teko was intending to stay there for six months but ended up sticking it out for a year. His daughter was confused whenever she came over to visit. She could not understand why the playing area at her dad's house had shrunk.

'And these just aren't the kind of things you can explain to a six-year-old,' Teko recalls with a chuckle.

The media was having a field day with Teko's new lifestyle. That bothered him less and less, though. He was used to the media by this stage. What bothered Teko was the fact that his teammates had found a seat in the peanut gallery. They too began gossiping about him: 'You see, Teko is broke. The papers are right; the guy went from an M3 to a Jeep to a Golf. How else do you explain that?'

Teko heard it all. There was no escaping it. He persevered, though, and it added to the resilience of his character. Teko got to feel the effects of a downgrade. Since he had started making money, he had never gone backwards, so it was an important lesson to learn. He learnt what it would be like if he were to one day lose his money, and he was okay with it. He felt the pinch. He watched how rapidly fake friends left his life as soon as he moved into a smaller place. It was an exercise in filtration. When all the dust had settled and the money had been put out of sight, only the most genuine people in his life remained.

After Teko had stayed in the flat for a year, he felt he had learnt whatever lesson was needed. He called Jazzman and told him he thought he was ready to move back into a bigger place so that he could have family over to stay. Jazzman was supportive; he always is.

Teko moved out of his flat. People started slowly coming back into his life, although he was wiser now as to who was a genuine friend and who to keep at a distance.

Teko got a call one day from his friend who worked in a car dealership. Teko always bought his cars from the same dealership.

'Hey, Teko, I want you to come over here and look at this car.'

'What car is it?' Teko asked.

'No, if I tell you then you won't come.'

'Send me a picture of the car.'

'No, just come here and look, Teko.'

'Just tell me the brand at least.'

'It's a Jaguar.'

Teko began laughing, 'Listen, my friend. I am a footballer. I am not a white businessman. I can't be driving around in a Jaguar.'

'Just come drive this thing and see for yourself.'

It was the Jaguar F-Type – a car so slick and smooth that it seemed destined to be driven by the villain in a James Bond movie. Initially, Teko saw a white one and was not convinced. However, a little later on they brought in a maroon cabriolet. Teko fell in love instantly and bought the Jaguar there and then.

He was enjoying driving the Jaguar and listening to the way she rumbled and roared down the road. One day, however, when he was going away with a friend for the weekend, they couldn't fit their bags in the boot of the Jaguar, so he started making plans to sell it.

The day he was at the dealership selling the Jaguar, another car caught his eye. It was a Porsche GTS. Teko had never driven a Porsche before, but that very same day he drove home in it.

Teko's doctor was not the only one who counselled him this time. There were also a few occasions when Jazzman had to step in: 'Teko, understand this, my boy. I was never in this to make money off you. I have my other businesses already. I've been in your boots before. I've been a professional footballer. I could see people I played with, unbelievably talented players who today beg for petrol money every day. My man, I don't want that to happen to you. I want you to be well off after football. It's not about me. Don't worry about me. Just do what I tell you, my friend – you will be well off.'

Teko admits that without Jazzman's guidance he may have been bankrupt 10 years ago.

'I had an especially tricky job as his agent because Teko is a big spender by nature,' reflects Jazzman.

Every time Teko would stray away from the plan and be seen in a new, expensive car, Jazzman would have to rein him in again.

'My friend, you don't need people to see you in a big expensive car. As a footballer, you actually don't need a car. Half the time, you are in camp. The rest, you are in a bus or on a plane. When do you drive this thing that costs you R20 000 a month? Put that money somewhere else. If you need a car, buy a small car to go to work. When you go to training, that's you going to work. You don't even need a small car. You're a superstar – we can get you a sponsored car for free!'

Teko eventually came to appreciate Jazzman's cry from the heart. It took a while, though. Jazzman even had to take some of Teko's friendships into his own hands. In his darkest times, he attracted the most poisonous people.

'Teko, when your playing days are over, these people will no longer be around.'

As Teko moved on from his austere lifestyle he began buying all the nice things he could afford once again. He had beautiful watches, a house and a car, but there was one thing he still yearned for.

The one car Teko has always wanted is a VW Scirocco. One day he began looking on the market for one. That same day he got a call from Jazzman.

'Downgrade everything'

'Hey, boeti, VW want to sponsor you. They want to give you a car.'

He stopped looking for a Scirocco. VW handed him a Golf 7, a very nice car – it wasn't Teko's dream, though. The car was also a bit faulty and was giving Teko problems so he gave it back to them. In a meeting, he asked them, 'So can I have any car I want?'

The VW execs in their suits looked at each other and then at Teko in his swaggered attire. 'Yeah sure, Teko, any car you want. We want to drive the sale of cars in Soweto. We feel like you're the right ambassador to do that, so you get to choose.'

Teko drove out of that meeting in a shiny, new navy-blue Scirocco, and he didn't pay a single cent for it.

The downgrade taught Teko many things. He learnt that he is a survivor, he has been through worse and if the day comes when he has to live with less money, he will be okay. He learnt which people poisoned his life and who gave it potential. Most importantly, he learnt that you can take a day or two out of life in the fast lane, and everything will still work out fine. You may just find yourself driving your dream car without paying for it.

CHAPTER 24

Meant to be just friends

In the beginning of Teko's Sundowns career, he met a beautiful young woman, Lizelle Tabane, who would go on to turn his world upside down.

Teko confesses that he became a different person under the spell of her love. He was doing things that he still struggles to comprehend today.

'It was easy to give myself to her because she was a great person. I was genuinely in love with her. I saw only the good side of her.'

He opened up to her in a way he had never done before. Teko feels that maybe it was easier to fall in love with her because by the time they met he didn't feel as hurt or damaged from past experiences as he does today. Teko knows that it will be difficult to love someone else like he loved Lizelle.

Lizelle was never supposed to be Teko's girlfriend. They were meant to be just friends. A friend of Teko's was staying in a hotel in Sandton, and Teko stopped by to collect his sunglasses, which he'd left behind previously.

When Teko arrived at his friend's hotel room, he noticed a girl sleeping, in the middle of the day. It was Lizelle.

'Guys, were you that drunk last night that this chick here is still sleeping at three o'clock in the afternoon?'

They admitted that the night before had been a heavy one and decided it would be good to get dinner downstairs in the hotel.

When Lizelle woke up, she was exceptionally scruffy, but Teko didn't care; he wasn't even looking at her in that kind of way. She seemed far too young anyway.

Following that day, Teko and Lizelle became friends: she actually already had a boyfriend at the time.

Their friendship developed; she confided in Teko about many things, including her love life. One evening, she came to Teko's house to get dressed before she went out on a date night with her boyfriend. Teko had agreed to give her a lift to her date and after putting on a stunning dress she hopped in his car and off they went.

When they arrived at the meeting spot for her date, the man was nowhere to be seen. She tried to call him and there was no answer. Eventually the boyfriend ended up switching off his phone. Lizelle was embarrassed and hurt: 'It's fine, Teko, you can just drop me off here. I will find my way.'

'No ways, Lizelle. We are in the middle of Sandton, and your bag is at my house so you have to come back anyway. Let's just wait another 30 minutes and see.'

What followed was an extremely uncomfortable silence that seemed to stretch on forever. She tried to call her date over and over again and it became clear that he was not going to pick up.

'Let's just go,' she eventually said.

On their way back to Teko's house, they stopped at the garage to buy some soft drinks. Teko found that the cooldrink she asked for was not in stock so he went back outside to ask what else she would prefer. What he saw when he went back to the car changed the way he felt about women in general and Lizelle in particular.

She was sitting alone in the car crying. Teko turned around, deciding that buying her something was better than nothing. He got her some treats and they left. He never said anything.

'From that day, I said to myself that I don't want to ever be that guy. Seeing her cry changed everything. If I didn't see her cry, she would probably still just be my friend. I doubt we would have ever dated, but that moment changed it all. She had so prepared herself to be with this guy and she ended up crying like that. I saw her getting ready, putting on her makeup and putting in the effort. I decided that I never wanted to be that guy. Things became different from that day. Even when she went to break up with that guy I was with her.'

When Teko had married Felicia, it had felt very ordinary. Because she was pregnant he figured they should get married. There was no special ceremony or romance about it.

Teko remembers the moment when he proposed to Lizelle. He put in a real effort there. Teko was different with her. It was the first time he bought a girl flowers and took her out on date nights.

'With Felicia it was responsibility; with Lizelle it was love.'

The night Teko proposed to Lizelle, he made a scene of it. It was at his home; he cooked her dinner (among Teko's talents, he is also a decent chef). He never went down on one knee though. It was something that she would later tease him about. She did recognise how hard he tried to do it properly and even cried when he proposed. It was a great moment and the next day it was on Instagram. The right procedures were followed through: Teko sought permission from her family first and he paid the lobola to her father.

The relationship fell apart because Teko felt that the person she became was not the person he fell in love with. Once again, money got in the way. Lizelle wanted Teko to buy her a salon, one from a local franchise. He was about to do it too, but his trust issues got in the way once more and he hesitated.

'Okay, Lizelle, let's go 50/50 on this. Since you stay in my house, since you're going to be earning a salary here, why don't you go to the bank and take out a loan and buy yourself a house. So that if anything happens between you and me, you will have your own house. You and I are not guaranteed.'

'No man, Teko, don't curse us.'

She didn't want the 50/50 deal. Teko put his foot down at that point. He was not willing to buy her a salon because should anything happen between them, he would have to sit back and watch her make money off his investment. Money began to poison their relationship and it was a slippery slope that dragged them down.

Teko felt the difficulty and realised that if he were to go through with the marriage, it would not be long before he was divorced again.

Lizelle never fully saw the break-up coming; naturally, she was furious and felt let down. She didn't really know where to direct her anger, so she took their issues to the media.

Their break-up was awkward, even by usual standards. They were living together in the same house with her child. It was a big compromise on Teko's behalf that they decided to live with her child and not his.

In the midst of their break-up, one Thursday, Lizelle went out on a drinking spree with her friends, leaving Teko at home. During the girls' night out, more than a little tipsy, one contacted a journalist and they concocted a story. By Sunday, it was headline material in the newspapers.

The story hit the newspapers before Teko had time to inform his family that he was about to break off his engagement. He received many frantic calls from family members that day. They were very surprised at the news. On Monday, Lizelle called Teko, wanting to make amends.

'I've got nothing to talk to you about,' Teko told her. 'You've already said everything you want to say in the media, so what's the point?'

Lizelle persisted and Teko accepted.

Teko and Lizelle spoke for two hours. She spoke openly of her regrets about lying to the media. She said she felt bad; her friends had wrongly influenced her.

Teko listened to her and eventually said, 'Well, if you regret it so much then pick up the phone. Call that journalist, that very same journalist, and tell him what you're telling me now. Tell him that you lied.'

She refused to make the call. She did want Teko to take her back though, but he was too hurt for that.

'Go on and say what you want,' Teko told her. 'There is nothing worse that can be said about me. Go on and ride the wave like all those other girls; go see how far it takes you.'

The experience with Lizelle left Teko a wrecked man. Once again, he had to review the role that money and fame played in his life and how it affected his ability to create the family he craved.

CHAPTER 25

The legend from Barcelona

Johan Neeskens is a big name in world football, and even bigger in South African football. He, along with Ruud Krol, was part of the revolutionary Dutch team that finished as runners-up in the 1974 and 1978 World Cups. Johan Neeskens played 140 games for Barcelona. Funnily enough, Neeskens was reportedly sold by Barcelona in 1979 because he refused to hand the president of the club toilet paper when the president was in a sticky situation in the club bathroom. He was a phenomenal footballer, though. As a coach, Neeskens started off as the assistant manager of Holland, travelled around the world and ended up in Chloorkop as the coach of Mamelodi Sundowns.

Teko really liked Neeskens. Teko liked anyone who could talk football and Neeskens was fluent. In fact, he counts Neeskens as one of his best coaches. Sundowns had every reason to perform well under Neeskens but they did not. The players did not like him. Key players started picking up injuries before crucial games. There was excuse after excuse and the team was falling apart. Mamelodi Sundowns looked to be in real danger of being relegated to the second division.

During Neeskens's tenure as the Sundowns coach, a hilarious incident played out when Mamelodi Sundowns were due to take on Teko's former love, Orlando Pirates, in November 2012. There was a kit manager at Sundowns named Freddy who was good friends with Teko. Freddy was nervous for the upcoming game. He was a superstitious man himself and he had heard the stories about the Pirates and their muti. Freddy thought that Sundowns stood no chance against the Pirates and their sangoma. He figured that defeat was a certainty unless they could match Pirates on a supernatural level.

Freddy decided to take matters into his own hands. While the players were in the change room before the game, Freddy casually walked out onto the field and was caught on camera cracking eggs on the halfway line.

The players were in hysterics when they found out about this after the game. The game was at three o'clock in Soweto. It was very hot so Teko approached Freddy after the game and joked with him, 'Hey, my friend. Were you trying to fry eggs or something? We know it was hot there on the field but you didn't have to try make breakfast on the halfway line!'

'No man, Teko, I knew that Pirates were going to use muti. I was scared so I was going to use some eggs to counter their muti.'

'Eggs!' Teko laughed. 'No, chief, I've never heard of anyone using eggs for muti. I think you were trying to make breakfast.'

That was a light-hearted moment in an otherwise sour period with the legend from Barcelona as the head coach. The junior players liked Neeskens and were ready to learn from him, but some of the senior players were having none of it. They really wanted to show Neeskens that this was their club and not his. Sundowns were playing Bloemfontein Celtic in the 2012 Telkom Knockout Final in Durban. They played entirely with youngsters as some of the senior players hadn't made the trip. Sundowns lost the game 1-0. Neeskens could see that his own players were sabotaging his job but there was little he could do about it. Neeskens and Teko spoke often, discussing Neeskens's real disappointment in the state of South African football.

It was not all bad for Neeskens, though. One of his achievements was a record-breaking 24-0 victory over a team called Powerlines FC. Yes, 24 goals in one game. The commentator in charge of the game quipped at the time, 'This game is like watching someone taking candy from a baby ... Except I know babies who can put up a better fight than this.'

That was, however, a brief moment of sunshine in an otherwise gloomy era for Sundowns and Neeskens. Later on in his tenure, Neeskens approached Teko with a question, 'Hey, Teko, who is Pitso Mosimane?'

Teko went on to explain the significance of Pitso and how he had worked with him before.

'Oh, okay,' Neeskens replied. 'I only ask because he wants to come here to coach Sundowns.'

Teko was confused by this. 'How does he want to come here and coach Sundowns when you are still the coach?'

Neeskens was not bothered by it at all. 'I don't know, but it's what I have heard. This is football; there are many things you can't control and you must just let them be.'

The writing on the wall was becoming bigger and clearer. Sundowns lost 2-1 to Maritzburg United. The supporters started chanting 'Neeskens must go!' and asking for Pitso Mosimane. They tried to break the stadium fence to get into the change room. The police managed to restrain the crowd that time, but a few weeks later, the police were no match for the mob.

It all came to a head during one league encounter when the fans attacked Neeskens. The week before, they had thrown objects at him from the stands after a loss. This week, Sundowns had lost a fourth game in the season; it was against Moroka Swallows. After the game, the supporters began throwing cans, bottles, broken chairs and food at the technical team.

This is nothing new in South African football and the standard procedure is for the players and the coaches to make a run for the change room as soon as tempers start flaring in the stands because things can get really ugly. This time, however, before Neeskens could get away the supporters managed to breach security and make it onto the field.

They caught Neeskens in the tunnel before he could make it to the change rooms and began to attack him. The police tried to flank him but there was little they could do. Video footage shows

Neeskens crouched down and covering his head as he tried to withstand the force of all the blows from angry supporters.

To Neeskens's credit, he did not quit after that. Mamelodi Sundowns were third from the bottom of the log and their players had to leave the field escorted by police on most days. While Neeskens may have had the stamina not to be deterred by the mob beating, Mamelodi Sundowns did not have the patience to give Neeskens more time. Billionaire South African owner of Sundowns Patrice Motsepe is a man of action, and one day he stood up in a press conference and announced that Johan Neeskens had been relieved of his duties at the club but Sundowns were nonetheless thankful for his efforts: 'Our current position on the log is extremely embarrassing and we have to restore the dignity and pride of Sundowns and its supporters. I am excited to welcome Pitso Mosimane to Mamelodi Sundowns.'

Teko had seen this coming for a while. He knew that there was no way Neeskens was going to last. In fact, such is the cruelty of the situation that when it was announced to the players that Pitso Mosimane was the new head coach, Neeskins was still in the building collecting his papers.

Teko recalls. 'The players did not like him; he was too straightforward, too European, too angry, too loud.'

Neeskens came across like an angry colonial missionary to the players. The player power at Sundowns was truly frightening. There can only be one boss in the change room, and if the players have the capability of getting a coach fired then you know where the power lies. Neeskens came in and wanted to change everything; he wanted to implement everything he had learnt at Barcelona. His problem was that the players were not willing to listen. Neeskens packed his bags and walked out the door at Chloorkop.

CHAPTER 26

Pitso is in the building

The ground shook as the door swung open at the home of Mamelodi Sundowns, Chloorkop. The players tapped their feet nervously and stared down at their hands. Everyone was on edge. Pitso Mosimane had arrived.

The sound of Pitso's footsteps down the hall for the first time meant a couple of things. Firstly, it meant the holiday was over – Pitso was here to work hard, especially as the club was facing relegation. Secondly, it meant there was a new boss in town, not just another coach, but someone really in charge. It meant that the players were no longer calling the shots like they could under Neeskens. Pitso was an African. This meant that the players could not gossip about him, because every language they spoke, he understood. He even spoke fluent Greek. He knew South African footballers, he knew the players, and he knew their habits. He knew everything, and he was here to make a point: there was no hiding from hard work now that Pitso was in the building.

Most of the Sundowns team had never worked with him, but Teko knew him all too well. He warned the other players: 'Now you guys are going to work. You think the tactics you used with Neeskens will fly with Pitso? Never. You think you can fake injuries with Pitso? Never. You think you can pick and choose games with Pitso? Never. This guy will tell you straight, he's not like Neeskens. He will tell you what's on his mind in front of the whole team. You guys think this will be easy? Never. We are 16th on the log, which means we are about to be relegated. Pitso is here for one reason and one reason only and that is to help us survive.'

The main thing that was rattling the nerves of the players and staff was the unpredictability. Pitso was an unpredictable coach and an emotional guy. You just never knew what trick was going to fall out of his sleeve next.

This was especially troubling for Teko. Pitso and Teko had gone through stages of liking and disliking each other, but one thing that had been constant was their respect for each other. They were two legends of the game in their own right. It was Pitso who had originally tried to sign Teko to SuperSport United, and it was Teko who decided to run away without saying a word. It was Pitso who did eventually sign Teko, and then drop him, telling Teko he would never play for Bafana Bafana unless Pitso said so. Pitso was the strict father, pushing and pulling at Teko. Teko was the energetic son, who was caught between trying to run away from him and trying to prove him wrong. Now Pitso was at Sundowns as the coach and Teko was the captain – both recovering from being shown the door at their previous places of employment. Pitso had just been relieved of his duties as Bafana Bafana coach after some dismal results and embarrassing moments. This relationship was either going to burn this club down to ashes or help them to eternal glory.

Pitso's first point of call was to change everything. He called his first team meeting and cut straight to the chase. This room was filled with the stars of the South African footballing world. He stood around the group of superstars and took a long time to look at all of them. These guys standing in front of Pitso had the deepest pockets and the biggest names in the game. He needed to show them who was boss.

'I see what has happened at this club,' Pitso said. 'Some of the older players and so-called established names have become complacent.'

He was right. Everybody knew it; Teko knew it. Between these players, they had maliciously got a Barcelona legend fired. In the process, however, they had shot themselves in the foot. They were lying 16th on the log, and suddenly it was no joke. Now they had to put their egos aside and listen to the new coach. He was their only hope.

In that first meeting, Pitso told the squad that he was going to sign 18 new players. This is an astonishing statement to make. He sounded like a madman. Signing 18 new players meant that he was signing an entirely new squad. He said he wanted to sign two or three players for every position. From the sounds of things, he would even change the badge, kit and ball boys if he could. They thought he was joking. He wasn't joking; Pitso doesn't joke ...

The message was loud and clear: the competition is coming; you better step up to the plate or get comfortable dusting the bench with your backside.

He brought in the best in the business: Katlego Mashego, Cuthbert Malajila and Khama Billiat were among the recruits.

The next thing Pitso did was invite Teko to his house one afternoon. As usual, he got straight to the point, telling him he was taking the captain's armband away from him. He was nice enough to sugar-coat it at least. 'I want you to be free, Teko. I don't want you to play under the pressure of being the captain. At this stage, I just want you to enjoy your football.'

Teko didn't say anything. He just listened. But he found what Pitso was saying didn't really apply to him.

'Free?' Teko thought to himself. 'I've never been free; I've never played without pressure. I feel it all when I play; people expect so much of me, and there is nothing people can tell me about my game that I didn't already know. As soon as I walk off that field, I know exactly how many bad passes I had and I know every mistake I should have fixed. I play with statistics in my head. I've never been free.'

Teko figured that the real reason for Pitso taking the captain's armband away from him was because it is always easier to bench a player who isn't the captain. There is less explaining to be done. It didn't bother Teko too much, though. He doesn't hold grudges.

Pitso managed to stabilise the ship. He took the bunch of players that were lying 16th on the log and managed to help them

The Curse of Teko Modise

to a ninth-place finish. It wasn't an immediate turnaround, though. At first, Sundowns still struggled and their confidence was lower than their league position. Pitso was not spared from the wrath of the supporters either. He too had to be escorted off the field in the back of a police van after angry supporters threw bottles and rocks at his head.

He is a resilient character, though, and made it through those tough times to help Sundowns avoid relegation. He didn't do it all by himself; it was a fantastic team effort that saw all the soldiers pulling together to win a very tough war.

The season was over and now it was really time for the Pitso way to take hold. Now he had a full pre-season to prepare his troops and get them playing the way he wanted. Teko was growing frustrated once more; he felt like all of Pitso's criticisms were being aimed at him. Every wrong pass, every missed tackle, every fluffed shot; it was all blown out of proportion. A Teko mistake seemed 10 times as costly as a mistake from anyone else in the team. Maybe it was because he expected more from Teko, maybe not. Only Pitso can really answer that.

Teko felt as if he was once again in the same position he had found himself in at SuperSport United. He felt that issues from their past had never been resolved and now he was paying the price for it. When the season finished and Sundowns were preparing to go on a pre-season camp in Zambia, Teko called Jazzman.

'I want to leave Sundowns,' he said. 'I'm not happy here; this is not going to work. Let's find a new home.'

Jazzman could hardly believe his ears.

'But … You wanted to leave Pirates? Now you want to leave Sundowns? You will get a reputation as a runaway player. When are you going to stay and face your devils? Where are you going to go? You are contracted to Sundowns. No one will buy you.'

It was not the first time Jazzman has had to remind Teko of the realities of life. In recalling the difficult times in Teko's life; Jazzman pauses, clenches his fists and pulls them closer to his chest. 'I had to remind Teko to hold on tight, keep it together, things will get better.'

Jazzman had been right in the past, things did start to get better then and he was right now too. Teko jetted off with Pitso and Sundowns for the pre-season.

A pre-season is a very important thing in football. It is the opportunity for the coach to see what weapons he has in his arsenal, for his players to get fit, for the team to get to know each other, and for everyone to figure out what their odds of winning the season are. For Sundowns, those odds were not looking good, given the outcome of the pre-season.

Zambia is a powerhouse in southern African football and its players are among the most talented on the continent. But a team with the infrastructure, talent and financial backing of Mamelodi Sundowns should have no problem beating these neighbours.

In Zambia, Pitso tried to change the whole face of the team. He wanted no ghosts from the season past. That season had been a disaster and he was willing to do anything to avoid that happening again. He tried out new combinations with the new, bright and shiny players he had bought. It all backfired like an 18th-century pirate pistol.

Sundowns lost all their games in the pre-season tournament. They prepared well for their final game of the tournament, determined not to lose every match. However, football has no feelings, and Sundowns lost their last game too. The most unfortunate part about it was that the player Teko was supposed to mark managed to break free of him and score a header in that final game. Pitso was furious.

Pitso is a very analytical coach, so after the latest disaster he showed the players the match video and pointed out every mistake, from the way the grass was cut to the goal Teko was meant to prevent.

The problem in Zambia was apparent and the whole team was nervous. Things were going from bad to worse for Sundowns. They couldn't win in South Africa and they couldn't win outside South Africa either. There was nowhere to go. The players were well aware that they had escaped relegation by a margin as big as their toenails. They knew of millions of rands poured into the club by Patrice

Motsepe and various sponsors. Most importantly, they knew that there were thousands of supporters' hearts whose happiness rested upon their performance. They knew that all these things were on the line and they were not in a position to better themselves. Like a bride spilling red wine on her white dress, losing all your games in pre-season is nothing short of a disaster.

Spirits were low and the players were solemnly packing their bags, getting ready to leave Zambia. A team meeting was called. The players dropped their bags and dragged their feet back to the meeting room. Pitso stood at the front and waited for everyone to be seated.

'Somehow, overnight, they have scheduled a friendly for us today. One last game before we leave Zambia.' Pitso scanned the room. He too was deflated, he too just wanted to get on the plane and fly away from this nightmare. 'I'm not going to select a team. Whichever of you feel like playing can play.' He scanned the room again and repeated himself: 'Whoever feels like playing can play.'

Everyone was exhausted. Teko was exhausted. It had been a long, gruelling trip with little reward, and everyone was reluctant at first. But Teko put up his hand and proudly stated that he would play. This in turn caused a number of other players to raise their hands and commit to go to war beside Teko.

That game on that day in hot, humid Zambia changed the face of Mamelodi Sundowns forever.

The squad of self-selected players happened to be most of the players that Pitso was trying to phase out of the squad, the good-for-nothing, leftover, expired superstars of yesterday. Well, they played one of the best games you will ever see in the yellow and green colours of Sundowns. It was no easy game; it was a battle, two giants going toe to toe. Zambia is hot and the earth is dry. Teko and the troops managed to win the game. It was their first and only win of the whole tournament.

Pitso could hardly believe his eyes and a shift occurred in his brain. He is a smart coach and he recognised the fighting spirit he saw in front of him. He decided to keep the core of that team, including Teko, together and take them back to South Africa for the new season.

That same team started off their campaign with a sublime 10-match unbeaten streak. Teko was simply phenomenal. The General was back – he made the entire team tick. His passes were frighteningly accurate; he slithered the ball in between defenders like a thread through the eye of a needle. He was meticulous and careful, yet explosive and ruthless at the same time. He looked younger than ever.

Teko took his opportunity at Sundowns by the horns. He had earned his stripes at Pirates, now it was time to do it at Sundowns.

Teko was a vital member of that team, particularly when the second half of the season arrived and characters were truly tested. Teko scored the second goal in a game against AmaZulu in Durban, securing the league title for Mamelodi Sundowns. Teko scored an absolute stunner against Kaizer Chiefs from the halfway line in a 1-0 victory. On the day that the league finished, he scored against SuperSport United from outside the box, striking the ball with so much power that it shot to the top-right corner of the goal.

Teko started scoring the kind of goals that he doesn't usually score. He was putting away goals with his head, goals from the halfway line, any kind of goal you could think of. He became a truly different player for Mamelodi Sundowns.

Later, when the season was over, Pitso had something to admit: 'Football has taught me a lesson. It has taught me that you should never, ever write people off.'

That same Sundowns team that won the final game in Zambia went on to win the league that season. Those players who lifted the trophy had been deemed expired goods before the season, Teko included.

Suddenly there was less to write about the 'Curse of Teko'. He had been instrumental in bringing all Sundowns opponents to their knees and making them bow before the Brazilians. For once, he was the best player and the team was also in the best position. The General was at his peak.

Following their successful campaign, Pitso had to take a long, hard, inward look. In front of him was a group of dedicated men willing to go to hell and back for their team. In front of him he had a group of players who had managed to survive relegation and go on to win the league. In front of him he had Teko Modise.

Teko, too, had massive appreciation for Pitso, despite their differences. They had been through a lot together.

'To win all these things with Pitso was amazing. I know how Pitso fought for me to play for him. He tried to get me when I was 19. He tried again with City Pillars; he had to work really hard to find my clearance. He saw my growth as a footballer. He was even the one who advised me to go to Orlando Pirates. He had to come back from the bottom after being fired from Bafana Bafana. For him to come back and win with Sundowns, win with me, despite our differences, is truly amazing. I want to thank him for everything he has done for me. If there is one coach who has been with me consistently throughout my career it is him. I think sometimes Pitso and I forget our similarities. At the end of the day, he knows that he can always count on me. If Pitso needs a soldier, he knows to send me in. So, for me to see him go on to win the African Coach of the Year, as a black South African … It means a lot to me.'

Teko has played some of his happiest days at Sundowns. He rediscovered the joy of football with them in that first season. It was such a huge relief for him that finally the apparent curse had disappeared. Teko meant to celebrate but he was honestly too exhausted.

On the bus on the way back after the game Teko received a call from his sister, Kgomotso: 'I'm so happy for you, Teko. I'm so happy you finally won. I know it means a lot to you to win the league and to win it like this. People don't appreciate you and the talent you have. You have done so much for South Africa, I'm really proud of you.'

It was one of the happiest moments of Teko's life, lifting the league trophy. Over the years he had won many individual awards. This year was no different as he won Gauteng Sports Personality of the Year 2014. His real achievement, though, was winning with his team. Teko had won so many awards but he had never had the opportunity to be on the podium with his team.

Teko remained at Mamelodi Sundowns for six years. It was a very fruitful time. The club became more ruthless, unstoppable and unimaginably poetic in the way they played football. Perhaps Teko's greatest achievement with the team came towards the end of his career in 2016.

The CAF Champions League is an African version of the UEFA Champions League. It has the same structure in the sense that it is a competition involving the best clubs from each country on the continent. South African teams do not have a good track record in this competition. It is worth stating that the conditions players must face in this competition are unlike anything experienced anywhere else in the world. Africa is no easy place to travel and the locals are not particularly welcoming when the purpose of your visit is to beat them in a game of football.

The only South African team to win the tournament had been Orlando Pirates in 1995. Since then, many teams had either been knocked out early or had chosen to be knocked out early because the conditions were too tough and risky.

Mamelodi Sundowns did not enter the competition with great expectations in 2016, and not much was expected of them in return. They had just won the local PSL league title for the second time in three years, and while that was a great achievement in itself, they wanted to test themselves against the rest of the continent.

Each game in the CAF Champions League consists of two matches – home and away. In Sundowns' first game they were drawn against Chicken Inn FC of Zimbabwe. The boys were fired up and ready to show the continent what they were made of. Unfortunately, they lost. Sundowns were kicked out of the competition at a very early stage.

This meant that the players could now make holiday plans with their families because they had more time off thanks to being eliminated early from the competition.

This relaxed holiday break did not last long, though. Mamelodi Sundowns received a call one day informing them that one of the other teams in the tournament had been disqualified over some technicality. The message was clear: 'Cancel your holiday plans, dust off your boots and report for training.'

This was a huge development; it is not often the case in football that you get a second chance to make good on your previous mistakes.

Teko and some of the senior players in Sundowns had a conference upon hearing the news. They decided that they should give this competition everything they had. For too long, South Africa had been shielded from international competition. It had been many years since the South African football supporter had something to smile about. Sundowns had won the league, but that proved nothing. Would they still be one of the bigger fish in a bigger pond? The older players of Sundowns decided that the best way to justify their readmission would be to try to go all the way and become the first South African team to win the Champions League in 21 years and the second one to do it at all.

This competition serves as a true test of character and that is not only because of the quality of African players on the field. It is because of the off-the-field tactics. Many African countries will try to win the game before the first whistle by deterring their opponents with unliveable conditions, intimidation and violence.

Mamelodi Sundowns were prepared. Under the guidance of Teko and the other senior players, they decided that everyone was willing to put in the work and fight like a soldier until the job was done.

Their first real test came when they were playing away in the Democratic Republic of Congo – one of the most hostile countries to visit as a footballer. The game was scheduled for late in the afternoon, and this was a concern for Sundowns because of what was happening in the country at the time. They had been warned that they needed to be out of the country by six o'clock in the evening because the general presidential elections in the DRC were set for the next day. These elections can be accompanied by much violence and unrest and the entire country would have a complete shutdown the next day. No travel would be permitted in or out, including that of Mamelodi Sundowns if they did not move fast enough.

After the match, they drove through the night on the team bus. Teko recalls it being a particularly dark drive with no street lights. They had no idea where they were heading. They had well and truly missed the six o'clock deadline for leaving the country; now they had to move on to Plan B: finding somewhere safe for the team to hide out. Election time meant that nobody was to be on the streets. The bus drove through the night for six or seven hours until they reached a different province. As the team had not planned to be spending the night, they did not have a hotel pre-booked so had to find the first one that was available.

The hotel was hardly welcoming or comfortable, but it was good enough given the circumstances. The players arrived at the hotel at around two o'clock in the morning. They all slept and when they woke up they felt like they were in a different world. The telephone lines had been disconnected across the country so no phone calls in or out were permitted. The signal for cellphones had also been cut, and there was no Wi-Fi. When Teko peered out the window of the hotel onto the street he noticed that the place was deserted. No one dare roam the streets on Election Day. The only people out in public were soldiers, fully dressed in uniform and armed with aggressive-looking machine-guns.

Whether Mamelodi Sundowns liked it or not, they were staying put. The flights coming in and out of the country had been cancelled for two days.

Eventually, the team was permitted to leave the country. The challenges they faced in that country was possibly the best thing for the boys. It drew them closer together and they figured that if they could survive conditions like those and still win on the field of play they could survive anywhere.

One of their biggest challenges was the state of the pitches they were playing on. Far from the manicured lawns of South Africa, the team struggled to adapt to a professional field complete with rocks, sand and bumps. Mamelodi Sundowns is a modern football club that plays a short, passing game with the ball on the ground. This is extremely difficult when the field is not straight, flat and covered in lush grass. However, they persevered and kept winning games due to sheer determination.

Mamelodi Sundowns also had to play a team from Algeria named ES Sétif, a well-known continental powerhouse. Sundowns were on fire that day and the game was heading for a 2-0 victory for the South African club. The Algerian fans had apparently not seen their team dominated like that in many years; they felt disrespected by the way Mamelodi Sundowns were outplaying their team so they disrupted the game by throwing bottles on the field, not particularly trying to hit, or miss, the players. The game had to be abandoned and the Sundowns players had to dash for the safety of the change rooms before being awarded the victory.

The most momentous part of the tournament was the climax, when Mamelodi Sundowns surpassed all expectations and reached the final. In the semi-finals, they faced off against Zesco United of Zambia and won 3-2 on aggregate after initially losing 2-1 in the first match.

The final, like the other games, had to be played over two legs, one in South Africa and one away. Sundowns' opponents were Zamalek, the most feared and successful club in Africa, with a daunting support base in Egypt. Incidentally, they also happen to share the nickname and colours of a famous South African beer, Black Label.

Zamalek has won more CAF trophies than any other team. Their supporters are among the most hostile and their style of football is simply uncontrollable.

The first match in Pretoria was like a dream. Mamelodi Sundowns put on a masterful performance for the home crowd. Most experts in the football industry agree that the crowd that day was the biggest ever assembled under the colours of Mamelodi Sundowns. The game finished 3-0 to Sundowns. It was the picture-perfect way to round off the tournament.

After the game, Teko walked over to the Sundowns supporters to thank them for coming out and singing. The fans always ask Teko for his shirt and this time he obliged. Teko excitedly threw his match jersey into the crowd, but it ended up having the opposite of the desired effect. A massive brawl and semi-stampede broke out. The police had to separate the angry crowd and Teko's iconic number-10 jersey got ripped clean in half. Teko felt he had to publicly apologise for the incident.

Even though Mamelodi Sundowns had demolished their Egyptian opponents, the job was far from finished. Sundowns still had the not-so-small matter of travelling to Egypt and hoping that Zamalek did not return the favour.

In Egypt, the supporters, players, army and country as a whole rally together to create the tensest environment for footballing visitors.

The entire stadium filled the eye with the red, white and black colours of Zamalek. There was a small, lonely crowd of around 140 Mamelodi Sundowns supporters looking very lost. The president of Mamelodi Sundowns, Patrice Motsepe, very generously footed the bill for this group of supporters to come and watch Sundowns do battle in Egypt.

The atmosphere in the stadium was unlike anything any of the players had ever seen before. Even Teko, with all his experience, was in shock.

'I've played in every competition there is. I've played in the World Cup, but that day in that stadium in Egypt was just something else. It was just amazing. Amazing and scary at the same time.'

All the Sundowns players had their phones out and were filming the crowd.

Things were not easy leading up to the tournament. Teko had received many threats from the Egyptian supporters in the build-up to the final. Many of them threatened to kill him and his family. One he received on social media read: 'You have two choices, death or lose … in Cairo you have no other choices.'

It didn't stop there. Even when the Mamelodi Sundowns players were still wearing their suits and walking around the field for the pre-match pitch inspection, the supporters started throwing glass bottles and other objects at them. During the game, Sundowns goalkeeper Denis Onyango was substituted off with an injury and was replaced by fellow goalkeeper Wayne Sandilands. Wayne did a great job of absorbing the pressure and protecting Sundowns' goal during the match. At one point during the final, the ball went out and Wayne moved to the side to fetch it. As he swooped down to pick up the ball, one of the ball boys sprayed his eyes with an unidentified substance. Wayne's eyes burned uncontrollably. The cameras never caught the incident but few can forget the sight of Wayne crawling back towards his goal and pouring the water from his bottle into his eyes in an effort to see again.

Sundowns defended their way through the 90 minutes of the game, and at the end they lifted the CAF Champions League trophy and made history as the first South African team in 21 years to win a continental competition, let alone the biggest continental competition.

It was an important lesson for the Sundowns players. They had the most advanced facilities, coaches and resources on the face of the continent and they were taught that skill may win you a game or two here and there, but heart and character are how you lift a trophy. Tough situations require tough people and Mamelodi Sundowns were truly fearless, carrying the South African flag with distinction.

The Sundowns players could hardly celebrate that night; they were too far away from home. The enormity of their achievement only set in when they landed back at OR Tambo International Airport in Johannesburg and were welcomed by government ministers, local celebrities and thousands upon thousands of supporters. They had won the biggest trophy a South African club could win.

In the Champions League final, Mamelodi Sundowns were under massive pressure in both the home and away legs. The General was sent in to control the pace. He slowed both games down completely and ensured that Sundowns kept the bulk of the possession. He laid the foundations for the other players to thrive and score and eventually make history by winning the Champions League. After their first Champions League encounter against Zamalek in the group stages, Teko was named in the best African XI for that period.

The home leg of the final was something special for Teko and

Pitso is in the building

for the rest of the Sundowns players. It was the biggest home crowd that Mamelodi Sundowns have ever played in front of. The stadium was painted yellow and green; there was not an empty seat in sight. Teko said to his teammates that day, 'Guys, look around. Even if we don't win this, we have changed the game forever.'

CHAPTER 27

The sun goes down

The honeymoon period of the CAF Champions League victory drew to a close and reality set in. It was becoming clear that there was less space for Teko at Sundowns. He was getting much less game time than he thought he deserved.

Public speculation regarding Teko's future at Mamelodi Sundowns was at an all-time high. Teko represented, at the time, one of the last bastions of a talented generation of footballers. With every passing year, the football community must bid farewell to a legend and with that legend goes the memory of his generation's greatness. To see Teko retire would be a sobering moment for the South African football lover. Yet, at the same time, at 34 years of age he was in no position to be demanding a starting place in the country's most skilful, expensive, youthful and competitive club.

As Teko's contract ran to a close, he was faced with a situation that was out of his control. Mamelodi Sundowns, if they so wished, had the option to extend his contract by one more season. If they were to refuse that then the public was waiting to pull Teko either back to Orlando Pirates or to arch-rivals, Kaizer Chiefs, with an outside chance that he may join an exciting new team called Cape Town City.

Although Teko had wanted to leave Sundowns for a while, he also wanted to give them a chance because he loved the supporters so much, but he didn't want to end his career watching from the bench as others played football. Teko had been searching for certainty in his future for a while and it was difficult to get clarity. Eventually Teko made up his mind: 'Jazz, let's organise a meeting with these people. I want to leave Sundowns.'

The meeting was no small deal. Teko had been at Mamelodi Sundowns for six years and was adored by the fans. Teko's difficulty with Mamelodi Sundowns was not the fact that he was being played less often as he got older; that was to be expected in the footballing world. What confused Teko was that he was under the impression that he was the back-up midfielder should anything happen to any of the younger players. However, instead of using Teko for the midfielder he is, the coaching staff were trying to convert players in other positions, such as defenders, into midfielders, using them as back-ups ahead of Teko.

Teko felt as if he was being tested.

Mamelodi Sundowns faced the same problem that most teams Teko played for faced – the supporters loved him. The implication of this is that, even if the coach didn't need him on the field, keeping him around was in the best interest of public relations. Teko was therefore always around on the bench but never quite playing. They kept him close but not too close and Teko grew tired of feeling like a brand ambassador.

'I realised that either myself or Pitso had to go. It was clear that he wasn't going anywhere. I was not in a position to disrespect him because, firstly, he is a father, secondly, he is a coach, and thirdly, he is a legend of South African football so to disrespect him would be to disrespect the team and I couldn't do that, so I decided to leave.'

Teko felt that Pitso's criteria for player selection was inconsistent. He would put Teko on for 10 minutes in one game; Teko would change the outcome and win the game and the next week he would not even be put in the squad. And despite their shared history, Pitso did not have a conversation with Teko for two years.

'We never spoke. The only time we spoke to each other was to greet each other. This is a person I saw every day of my life. You see your coach more than you see your kids, and we never had any kind of conversation. I could have a conversation with anyone in the team but him. There is a tension between Pitso and me that has been around for years and I will never fully understand it.'

Some of the other players used to notice the issues between Teko and Pitso and used to come and joke with Teko, 'Hey, man, are you and Pitso dating the same girl or what?'

Teko began feeling really bad about the team; he felt as if he was being disrespected in training and matches.

'Jazzman, get me out of Sundowns. If I am here for any longer I will start swearing at the coach.'

Teko was eventually called into a meeting. It was a huge meeting. All the coaching staff were present. The board of directors was there too. This was a massive issue. Teko was a senior player with much influence and if he was boycotting training sessions, it spelled trouble for the rest of the team.

At the meeting Teko used the platform to vent his frustrations: 'You guys told me to play less so that the team can shine more. What is that? Which other player has been told that? Tell me one game in which I have played for Sundowns that I haven't given my 100% best? When have I not given my all? I train harder than everyone in the team and I train earlier and later than everyone. I feel like an outcast in this team that I have given so much for. I play for a team where the coach doesn't even speak to me, what is that?'

In the meeting, Pitso did not say anything. He simply jotted down notes with his pencil while Teko was speaking.

Teko is the kind of man who will keep fighting until the end, so even in the afternoon of his career with Sundowns he still made his case known. He still felt as if he should be playing football more.

A team official asked that Teko should get Jazzman to compile a DVD of Teko's highlights from the upcoming FIFA Club World Cup in Japan.

'But I am not even going to kick a ball in Japan?' Teko responded to the suggestion.

'No, Teko, you will, man; you will see.'

Mamelodi Sundowns jetted off to Japan and lost both of their

The sun goes down

opening games, (2-0 to Kashima Antlers of Japan and 4-1 to Jeonbuk of South Korea). Teko did not kick a single ball during the team's time there, as he predicted. The only positive from that tournament for Mamelodi Sundowns was Percy Tau's consolation goal in their 4-1 hammering at the hands of the South Korean's. The young Tau scored his first-ever goal for Mamelodi Sundowns with a beautiful left-footed strike from a stubborn angle and managed to find the top-right corner.

The flight home from Japan is a long one and Teko had much time to reflect. He figured that if a club official could embarrass him by ordering a DVD of a tournament in which he never featured, he was clearly no longer wanted. After that he thought he would make things easy for Mamelodi Sundowns.

'Guys, don't worry, we're cool. Give me my papers and let me go. I'm not trying to fight anybody, we're good. I've done my part in the team. You guys have helped me and I've helped you. Sundowns is a great team, but it's time to let me go. Our relationship is done.'

There was one training session in particular that broke Teko. He felt truly for the first time that he was no longer welcome at Sundowns.

Teko screeched the wheels of his car into Jazzman's office parking. He was so frustrated. Jazzman admits he has never seen him so distraught in his life. Teko had tears streaming down his face. Jazzman knew, unlike at the beginning of his time with Sundowns when Teko had wanted to leave, he had to take it seriously this time. Seeing Teko cry broke Jazzman's heart and he set about getting his player out of Mamelodi Sundowns.

'I remember that face. I had only ever seen that face on Teko twice. The last time was towards the end of Orlando Pirates. I knew I needed to take him seriously this time. I would be in the history books for killing off Teko's career if I didn't get him out.'

Jazzman had a plan for Teko, but it was not easy and Teko needed to buy into it.

'Okay, Teko, we will get you out of there, but you gotta listen to me word for word. If you don't listen to me then you are screwed. Here is what's going to happen; it's going to be just like the end of Pirates. They are going to make you train behind the goalposts. They are going to make you train with the juniors. It's going to be tough. The team that plays the matches from now on will not feature you. You will be with the B-team. You gotta stick with it. If they say there are five people scheduled for training, you must still report and be on time. If you do that, I will get you out. If you miss training once, then we have no leverage.'

To Teko's credit, he swallowed his pride and did it. To the very last day, he attended training at the club he wanted so badly to leave. Eventually, Jazzman got a call from a Mamelodi Sundowns official: 'Teko doesn't need to report to training tomorrow. You can come fetch his clearance; he is free to go.'

When Patrice Motsepe signed Teko to Sundowns, the club had not won the league in six years. After his arrival, they won the Absa Premier League twice, the Nedbank Cup, the Telkom Knockout, the CAF Champions League, and the CAF Super Cup. Regardless of what his relationship with his club was, Teko always remained a firm fan favourite at both Orlando Pirates and Mamelodi Sundowns.

Teko had an insignificant end to his time at Mamelodi Sundowns. There were no fireworks or balloons, no party and no parting gift. Even in the final game of the season, when it was becoming clear that Teko was leaving, he was not given a chance to say goodbye to the supporters who loved him so much. It's clear that this was very hurtful for Teko.

'In South Africa, we don't respect our heroes. If I was appreciated the way people say then I would at least be given five minutes in my last game to play, just to say goodbye to the supporters. Everyone knew it was my last game and the league was already lost so it didn't matter. I played for that team for six years. I played my heart out for that team. I won trophies for that team. I played in both finals of the historic Champions League. When I came to Sundowns, the first thing I was introduced to was the supporters. All I wanted was five minutes to play to say goodbye to them.'

Upon the emergence of the news that Teko would be leaving, one supporter named Sizwe wrote, 'My heart is broken. My soul is destroyed. I thought the contractual negotiations were going to yield positive results. Teko Modise leaving Sundowns is like a girlfriend breaking up with you while you still love her. I'm so devastated. I thought he was going to retire at Sundowns. No, this is not right; who will wear the number-10 jersey now?'

Even supporters from other clubs couldn't help but pour in tributes upon hearing the news.

'I am a Moroka Swallows fan, sadly so. But I will never forget this man tearing through my defence in Dobsonville. There were not enough swear words for me to throw at him, he was just breath-taking. Well done Donadoni, you were one of the best that ever did it.'

CHAPTER 28

Making history

As recently as the year 2015, Cape Town City did not exist. Before 2015, it was a completely different outfit named Mpumalanga Black Aces. In South Africa, unlike England, it is legal to purchase a football club, change its name, change its emblem, change its coach and even the ground staff but still retain that club's status (that is, premier or second division).

That is exactly what John Comitis did when he bought Mpumalanga Black Aces, relocated the team to Cape Town, kept 14 Mpumalanga Black Aces players and told the rest to find new employment. John Comitis is a Greek South African who co-founded Ajax Cape Town in 1999 with his brothers-in-law and co-partners, the Efstathios brothers. He sold his shares in 2013 and returned in 2016 to start Cape Town City.

John Comitis roped in former Bafana Bafana midfielder Eric Tinkler as the coach and they set out to achieve miracles. In their first season, Cape Town City won the Telkom Knockout Cup, a competition played between all 16 teams in the top-flight league. They led the league for a decent length of time but ended up finishing third in their first-ever season, an incredible feat.

In the off-season, controversy ensued. Coach Eric Tinkler up and left his post at Cape Town City to become the head coach of SuperSport United. John Comitis, a known risk-taker, decided to hire South Africa's highest-ever scoring striker, Benni McCarthy, as the new coach. It was Benni's first-ever appointment as the big man in charge of a club. Benni had played some beautiful football with Teko Modise for Bafana Bafana so they were no strangers to each other.

Teko had had his eye on Cape Town City ever since halfway through their first season. They played such beautiful yet lethal football and had a dynamite captain in the form of Lebogang Manyama.

Jazzman and Teko set out to work. Their main goal was to keep the whole thing quiet. John Comitis's budget was already stretched. He had just bought Bafana Bafana left winger Ayanda Patosi from a Belgian club, as well as a Bafana Bafana immortal in the shape of Benni McCarthy. Now he was supposed to buy the one-and-only Teko Modise? Only a madman would be so bold.

Jazzman will admit that John Comitis was not sure about Teko at all. He had heard so many stories about Teko being a team disrupter and a negative energy. Teko and Jazzman had nowhere to go and no club. There were many rumours in the media that Kaizer Chief and Orlando Pirates were interested. It was not true. No one wanted to buy Teko, not even Polokwane City. He was too old, too expensive, and had a questionable reputation.

The only club boss who was half listening to the proposition was John Comitis. So, Jazzman had two plans: Plan A – push Cape Town City right to the limit and get him a new contract; or Plan B – call a press conference and announce Teko Modise's retirement from professional football.

Teko was getting nervous. Jazzman was honest with him. The reality began to set in that perhaps Teko would no longer be a footballer. His options were slimming down by the day.

When Benni McCarthy was employed, Jazzman called John Comitis. He suggested that because Teko and Benni had played together they may be a good fit. John was honest with Jazzman: 'Teko is too old for my team. I don't have the budget for him, I'm sorry.'

Before Jazzman put down the phone he asked John for Benni's number, and that changed everything.

'Hi, Benni! Congratulations on the job.'
'Thanks, Jazzman.'
'Benni, listen. Teko Modise …'
'Today, Jazzman.'
'What?'
'Today. I want him. If he is available, bring him. I will make sure Teko plays for me. I don't care what happens. I will make sure John finds money for Teko Modise.'

When Teko and Jazzman flew into Cape Town on a Saturday morning in May 2017, they had to be as discreet as possible. Teko Modise, Jazzman Mahlakgane, John Comitis and Benni McCarthy, four of the most powerful names in the footballing world, all went out for a dinner at the Waterfront. Teko and Benni chatted football and old Bafana Bafana memories. John and Jazzman chatted business. At some point during the dinner, John turned to Teko: 'You're a great guy, Teko. I will do all in my power to have you in my team.'

At the dinner, Jazzman joked that if John gave Teko a contract then Teko must pick up the bill for the food. John ended up paying the bill anyway.

John's reason for organising the dinner was to see whether Teko was the kind of guy you could have a conversation with, who would fit into his team and make his other players feel comfortable. From a business perspective, Teko understood: 'He wanted to make sure he wasn't bringing someone in who was going to destroy all he had built. He wanted peace and harmony in his team.'

The following day, John's phone was off. They could not reach him by any means. Jazzman eventually turned to Teko: 'My friend, this deal is off. I know these things when they play out like this. I've seen this movie before. I can tell you that this deal is off.'

After that, Jazzman could not reach John as he was overseas. Two weeks went by without any contact at all from him. Eventually John called Jazzman and gave him his absolute bottom line, just how much he could really pay Teko. The General was okay with all the arrangements. He just wanted to play football. They signed on the last day of the transfer window, 30 June 2017. If the negotiations had not been concluded at that point, Teko would have had to announce his retirement the following day.

The number that appears on a footballer's back is a very personal and superstitious thing. Teko has worn all the famous numbers throughout his career. At Orlando Pirates, he wore the famous number-11 jersey, previously worn by Jabu Mahlangu. For Bafana Bafana, he scored many famous goals with the number 12 on his back. At Mamelodi Sundowns, he held the incredible honour of putting on the number-10 jersey and making it his own for six years. A jersey so legendary that it was presented to him by the Black Prince of South African football, Jomo Sono.

By the time Teko was signed to Cape Town City, all his meaningful jersey numbers were taken. He so badly wanted the number 10 but Ayanda Patosi had already got it strapped to his shoulders. They decided to give Teko the number-13 jersey. It is a tricky number to wear in a superstitious sport, and initially Teko was not pleased. But when it was pointed out to him that he would be the first-ever number 13 of Cape Town City he put it on with pride. The General continues to capture the history books.

What a fitting number for Teko to see out his career. The man whose mother thought he was bewitched, the man who carried a curse in the footballing world, the man who attracted a king from Congo ... The man who turned all these curses into blessings will now wear unlucky number 13, and he will set out to change the fortunes of that too. The number has already proved to be a blessing as the General scored on debut for Cape Town City in their 3-1 win over Platinum Stars in 2017. Teko has always made his own luck.

EPILOGUE

Not so cursed after all

This is an incredible story; much more than just a story about football, it is a truly South African story as lived by a man who has been exposed to the highs and lows of life in this country, and some almost unbelievable experiences.

On the football field, Teko's contribution, class and character will always be memorable. Teko Modise slowly changed from being just another talented young footballer to becoming an iconic and colossal brand and he did it all with guts and determination, and by standing on his own two feet. They just don't make footballers like Teko any more. His career has spanned over 16 years at the time of writing and in that time he has, remarkably, only received one red card.

Teko has stood the test of time and has done so because he learnt how to decide which temptations and offers to refuse. The more famous he became the more offers and promises he received. If you are ever fortunate enough to meet Teko in person you will be struck by his humility and respect, for football and for other people.

'If you don't respect football it won't respect you back. If you don't train hard, even the simplest things will become difficult. You will struggle to control the ball or make a pass. If you train with passion then football will reward you.'

Teko consulted the great Shoes Moshoeu on the matter of

staying power. Shoes managed to perform at the highest level up to the age of 40. Shoes confirmed for Teko that the biggest challenge in a game as physically, mentally and emotionally taxing as football is not talent but the endurance of talent.

Teko recalls, 'It breaks my heart. I see so many young boys with so much potential just thrown away. It is scary to see. The game of football has developed. It is no longer just about skill. Nobody cares if you can juggle a ball. Football is business. Football is science. What I have learnt in football and in life is to always listen to advice. Even if it is bad advice that you are given, listen anyway, if for nothing more than just out of respect. One day that same person who gave you bad advice may give you the best advice of your life. I listen to everybody, be it a footballing legend or a parking guard. I even listen to the petrol attendants when they give advice. I may even be in a bad mood or in a rush but I will still listen. At the end of the day, these people are the ones who support you and watch you week in and week out, so you are nothing without them. I listen to people because I've always wanted to be great. Since the beginning, I've always wanted to be better than Doctor Khumalo, so I kept my head down, worked hard and listened. I remember when I was at Orlando Pirates and things were not going well for me. I would have people, all kinds of people from all kinds of different places, come and visit me at training. There would often be pastors and their flocks from different churches telling me that they have come to save me. They would tell me that I would break one of my legs if I didn't do this or drink that. Even though I knew it wasn't true, I listened anyway.

'I still play like I have nothing. I still play like I've got no car; I play like I've got no food or no house. I play like I've got nothing. I play for everything. I don't ever want to be comfortable. You'll never hear me brag about material things or money. It was never about that when I started football. I just love the sport. When I was growing up admiring Doctor Khumalo, I didn't even know what car he was driving. I still don't know what he drives. I did know that he made people happy, though, just by playing football. Doctor is my icon. How many years has he been retired? And we

The Curse of Teko Modise

still talk about him today; he is still relevant. I want to be just like that. In a way, you know, Doctor Khumalo saved my life. I really mean that – Doctor saved my life. It was through him that I became obsessed with football; it was he who made me believe I could be great. I saw the joy he brought to the faces of the people in the township … I decided I wanted to be that shining light for people.

'I want to share my story so that people know they are not alone. There is definitely some footballer out there who has been through much harder times than me, but South African men tend to be too proud to talk about our problems. What people forget is that we are just human beings. We appreciate that people come to the stadiums and spend their hard-earned cash to watch us, but sometimes we will have bad days. We cannot be superheroes our whole lives. After the football game has finished, I'm just Teko. I'm a brother, a son and a father. I just wanna inspire the younger guys. I want them to know that the sky is the limit. I started on the street and ended up where I am today just by working hard and not giving up, no matter how difficult it got. I want those young footballers to know that they mustn't get down about the fact that they are not earning as much money as they expect or playing as often as they should. Trust me. I was recognised at the age of 26. That was the first time most people had ever heard of Teko Modise: 26. There is no formula or criteria for how to achieve success; all you can do is keep working hard because everything will happen in its own time. All you gotta do is be ready when it happens. No matter how tough things get, you gotta keep working towards your goals.'

To contextualise Teko's contribution to South African football, it is best to take the words of the man who knows him best – at times his mentor, at times his challenger, but always his admirer and colleague. As was reported in *Phakaaati*, Pitso Mosimane says, 'I am happy that if Teko Modise retires he can say, "I've won international tournaments, I have contributed." An unflagging player like Teko, I think he has ticked all the boxes. He played in the FIFA World Cup with the national team; he played in the African Cup of Nations with Bafana Bafana. He played the FIFA

Club World Cup, he played the CAF Champions League and won that ... The Confederations Cup too, what has he not played in?'

Teko has faced the same kind of temptations as many other superstars. He was offered everything from drugs to money to women. Teko will admit that he made many wrong decisions along the way, and that is understandable; he has been handicapped by having little guidance from his family and growing up without a father. One of Teko's greatest fortunes was that Jazzman came into his life.

'Jazzman has become my father. To be honest, we used to fight a lot. The biggest fight we had was when my overseas deal didn't happen. I remember going for months not speaking to him, not answering his calls or anything. My divorce proceedings changed my relationship with Jazzman. He helped me so much when no one else would. Since that divorce, he started going above and beyond for all his players. After that he was no longer just my agent; it was something special. That's why nowadays, when he asks me to do something, I will do it without questioning. Jazz is one of a kind. If there is a funeral in your city, Jazz will fly in. Any player that is his, he will do the same for. Any player. He treats everyone the same and that is what I respect him for. Because I never grew up with a father figure, it was special to have Jazz around. He is the only one. He is the only person who has been solid the whole time I have known him. He has been the most stable part of my life.'

There are many ways to quantify Teko's career on the field. You could count his numerous Man of the Match awards. You could see how many times he won Footballer of the Year or take note of the fact that he was the first one to win that award. You could count the number of times he has captained his team or the number of competitions he has played in. You could even tally up his goals, and all of the above would paint an impressive statistical picture of the contribution Teko has made to football.

However, the truest measure of the greatness of Teko Modise does not lie in the numbers, statistics or charts. His true measure of greatness lies in the hearts of millions of South Africans. His skill and effort on the field bring joy to everyone who watches him play. Even opposition fans have been caught clapping out of sheer admiration for the General.

What many non-sport lovers fail to realise is that football is not just a sport. Especially in South Africa. In a country where so many are unemployed and strangled by poverty, those 90 minutes when South Africans get to watch their idols battle it out on the field are some of the happiest times of their lives. Teko stated from the beginning of his career that he wanted to make it big in football because of Doctor Khumalo. He saw the joy that spread on people's faces when they spoke of the great Doctor, and joy is precisely what Teko has brought to anyone fortunate enough to watch him play.

Teko's football has been closer to art than sport. It is, in fact, the perfect blend of art and science. Teko Modise is a poetic engineer in the way he can control an entire football game, and we thank him for all he has done for our country and our hearts.

The off-the-field life of Teko Modise is just as remarkable. No matter your talent, it takes something special to graduate out of the hood and make a success of yourself. It is easy to forget that the superstar appearing before us on the television, driving fancy cars and living in lavish houses, was once just a poor, homeless boy in Soweto, eating out of dustbins.

Teko has had a truly eventful life up to this point, from his troubled upbringing to his difficult and public relationship issues, from his interactions with hard-to-fathom organisations to his supernatural encounter with a king from Congo. This is a man who purposefully gave up his riches to attract more genuine people into his life.

Teko has made his mark on this world and will live on in the South African memory. Most importantly, Teko has created a stable environment for his daughters, and his greatest achievement is that they will never grow up as he did.

Teko has constantly struggled with trust issues. All he wanted was genuine love, not a relationship built on his name or salary. He did eventually find it; in the little girl he calls his princess. Paballo Modise, Teko's daughter, seven years old at the time of writing, is wise beyond her years. She carries her father's proud attitude and sass, and she means the world to him.

'When I take my princess out and we are walking in a shopping mall, and people stop me to take pictures with me, she just carries on walking. The first time she did it, I ignored it. She kept doing it though, so one day I asked her why she never stops and waits when people take photos. She said to me, "I don't understand why people can't understand that this is my time with you. When you are there on TV and when you are playing football then the people can take pictures with you, then I know I have to share you with the world. But when we are here this is my time with my dad."

'My daughter is so smart. She is the one person who understands me better than anyone and I understand her perfectly too. I am trying to build the kind of relationship with my daughter that, no matter what happens, she won't ever be scared to come and talk to me. Once you feel you cannot speak to your parents, you start doing all the wrong things. I know, especially now in her growing years, I need to make sure I do a good job as a father. She's marvellous; she doesn't see me as Teko Modise the star, she doesn't even like taking pictures with me. She just wants to be around her dad. Just her and me, low key.'

There are many titles that have been given to Teko Tsholofelo Modise over the years. You may know him as the Navigator, or you may call him Google Earth. Others know him as Donadoni, named after a famous Italian footballer, with many just referring to Teko as the Don. Those who saw him in his prime will forever know him as the General, or even King Teko.

What you know him as is not important. What is important is that you know him at all. It is important that you know the story of this proud son of Africa who proved that there is no mountain too high to climb, that a life that began in poverty does not have to end in poverty, and that the absence of a father when growing up does not disqualify you from being a good dad yourself.

South Africans are fantastic storytellers, but poor history recorders; we thank you, Teko Modise, for allowing your story to be recorded and shared. Yours will go down as one of the greats in the South African history books.

The author, Nikolaos Kirkinis, with Teko Modise, Joburg, January 2017